LOST TOLEDO

DAVID YONKE

Published by The History Press
Charleston, SC 29403
www.historypress.net

Back cover: The 212-foot *City of Toledo* steamer was built in 1891 and plied Lake Erie and Lake Michigan until 1943. *Courtesy Toledo–Lucas County Public Library*; Lake Erie Park and Casino, which opened in 1895 in Toledo's Point Place neighborhood, featured a boardwalk, a roller coaster, slot machines and more. *Courtesy Toledo–Lucas County Public Library.*

First published 2015

Manufactured in the United States

ISBN 978.1.62619.570.7

Library of Congress Control Number: 2015941002

To the people of Toledo

CONTENTS

ACKNOWLEDGEMENTS

I am deeply grateful to the Toledo–Lucas County Public Library's Local History and Genealogy Department, whose vast and well-organized resources made so much of the research for this book possible—and enjoyable. In particular, I would like to thank Jill Gregg Clever, department manager, and Donna Christian for their help and kindness and Laura Voelz for going above and beyond the call of duty in finding and scanning so many historic photos.

It is an honor to include in this volume photos by John Gibbs Rockwood and Leslie Cusano, true artists whose excellent work has preserved timeless pieces of Toledo history. Thanks also to music aficionado John Henry, whose expertise and energy sorting through tens of thousands of photos proved invaluable.

Thanks go to my keen-eyed colleagues who helped polish these words: Jon Chavez, Carl Ryan, Dennis Bova, George Tanber, Sue Brickey and Tom Gearhart.

I am grateful to John Husman, Mud Hens historian, for his time and expertise; to Greg Shapiro for dusting off his archives of the Aku-Aku Polynesian Room; to Matt Markey for opening this door into Toledo's past; and to all who took time to share their memories.

And for her endless patience, encouragement and support, I am thankful to my wife, Janet. I could not have done it without you.

INTRODUCTION

In the thirty-four years that I've lived in Toledo, I've seen many changes. Old buildings have been razed, new structures have been built, businesses and organizations have come and gone and demographics have shifted. In some ways, the city seems to be a living entity—always on the move, constantly changing.

My tenure in Toledo is just a blip on the city's timeline. Toledo is a city with a long, rich and fascinating history. The region was part of the Great Black Swamp and home to Native Americans for countless generations.

Maumee River view, 2013. *Author's collection.*

French and English troops began using the Great Trail (now Detroit Avenue) during the French and Indian War beginning in 1754.

The area became a strategic site during the War of 1812, with battles on Lake Erie and at Fort Meigs. Settlers started buying land in 1817, and Toledo was founded twenty years later with the merger of two villages, Vistula and Port Lawrence.

Toledo is a port city, located at the mouth of the Maumee River, the largest river flowing into Lake Erie. Its waterfront location has played a pivotal role in the city's growth, from the early settlers who could reach the area by boat to the workers who built canals and railroads and the entrepreneurs who started businesses and opened factories.

There are many wonderful and informative books on Toledo history, and there are dozens of knowledgeable historians. Many of their books focus on specific areas—either a particular industry or sport, a time frame or a person. All are important and well worth reading.

Lost Toledo is somewhat different in that it covers a broad range of local histories, all linked by one common thread: they've vanished from the local scene.

There are chapters on famous and beloved department stores Tiedtke's, Lamson's and Lasalle's; the exciting but short-lived Portside Festival Marketplace; the Mud Hens stadiums, where such legends as Babe Ruth, Ty Cobb and Mickey Mantle once played; the Sports Arena, where elephants, rock stars and hockey players all roamed; ethnic neighborhoods where new immigrants found work and friendship; jazz clubs that were known around the world; an auto plant that gave birth to the Jeep; and theaters that were so ornate people felt like they were entering the Taj Mahal.

It is unlikely that there are any other history books that mention Casey Stengel, Tiedtke's, Rusty Monroe and the Goaldiggers in the same volume. But they are all part of Toledo history. They are all part of *Lost Toledo*.

I hope you enjoy reading these stories as much as I enjoyed researching and writing them.

David Yonke
Maumee, Ohio
April 19, 2015

1
TIEDTKE'S

A NEW WAY TO SHOP

On a cloudy Saturday in November 2014, hundreds of Toledo-area residents flocked to a local department store to see a slice of history come back to life. The star of the show? A 3,200-pound block of cheddar cheese.

The huge cheese wheel was displayed—then sliced and sold in pieces—at the Andersons store in West Toledo after store officials and executives from the *Blade* newspaper teamed up to revive a holiday tradition that had ended more than forty years ago with the 1973 closing of Tiedtke's department store.

The crowd jammed into the Andersons' aisles, standing shoulder to shoulder amid rows of potato chips, stacks of imported beer and tables piled with baked pies, craning their necks to get a glimpse of the cheese. Before the ceremonial first slice was taken, Paula Larsen, the store's "goddess of cheese," led the enthusiastic crowd in two rounds of Tiedtke's corny but catchy jingle, "Let's all go down to Tiedtke's; it's fun to shop at Tiedtke's!"

After Andersons and *Blade* officials offered a few words of welcome, the go-ahead was given to the store's cheesemongers, who began cutting into the five-foot-tall block of aged Wisconsin cheddar. The giant wheel was sliced and diced, cut into pieces and sold to eager buyers for $4.99 a pound.

The excitement and festive atmosphere were not just about a big hunk of cheese, of course. It was more about taking a trip back in time—down memory lane of the sights, sounds, smells and tastes that made Tiedtke's such a unique and popular place to shop.

Tiedtke's was more than a department store; it was a place filled with music, aromas and bargains. *Toledo–Lucas County Public Library.*

Above: Hundreds gathered at the Andersons store in November 2014 to see a 3,200-pound wheel of Wisconsin cheddar, reviving a Tiedtke's tradition. *Author's collection.*

Opposite, bottom: A giant wheel of cheese, shown here in the early 1950s, was one of the favorite annual holiday traditions at Tiedtke's. *Toledo–Lucas County Public Library*.

The downtown store was a destination point for Toledo-area shoppers for nearly eighty years, from its founding in 1894 until its closing in 1973.

Clint Mauk, the Toledo Rotary Club's historian, described Tiedtke's as "not just a big store, it was a meeting place, a mystical community of contented Toledo shoppers, and a beloved institution."

Charles and Ernest Tiedtke, brothers raised on a farm east of Toledo, started with a small storefront at 40 Summit Street, near Monroe Street, investing their combined savings of $350. They called it Tiedtke & Todd, thinking it was more impressive to have another business partner's name on the sign (even though Todd was just a fictitious figure).

The first customers were crewmen aboard the ships docked along the Maumee River, the broad and muddy waterway that cuts through the heart of downtown Toledo en route to Lake Erie and the Great Lakes. The Tiedtke brothers, typically working from 5:00 a.m. until midnight, would steer their boat alongside the freighters, climb aboard and take orders for groceries and

Above: Charles and Ernest Tiedtke started their business in 1894 by using this boat to deliver groceries to docked freighters. *Toledo–Lucas County Public Library*.

Left: Tiedtke & Todd opened its first store at 40 Summit Street in 1894 with an investment of $350 and built its business into a local legend. *Toledo–Lucas County Public Library*.

dry goods. Then they would head back to shore, load up the bales and bags and personally deliver the goods to the ships.

Their goal was to sell goods in volume, making a small profit on each article. "Even if we only make five cents on an item, if we sell enough, we are going to get there," Charles once told Ernest.

Sales were on a cash basis, and the Tiedtke brothers soon generated enough income to expand their business. They began selling more of their goods on land, hauling dozens of baskets of fruit and vegetables onto the sidewalk in front of their store in the morning and then hauling them back inside at night. They also began delivering groceries to homes in Toledo. By 1909, the brothers had a warehouse on Water Street and a team of horse-drawn wagons delivering groceries all over town.

In 1910, Tiedtke's moved into a six-story building at 408 Summit Street, just north of Adams Street, with seven acres of floor space. It would be the store's main home for the next six decades.

Shopping for food in the early 1900s was generally considered a chore, something that had to be done but nothing to get excited about. The Tiedtkes were determined to change all that, making their store a fun place to shop, with a vast array of entertaining sights, sounds and smells, along with discount prices.

In the sprawling new building, Tiedtke's began roasting its own brand of coffee and grinding the beans in a high-traffic area of the first floor, giving customers a chance to see, hear and smell the coffee. Other stores ground their beans in back rooms or during off hours, thinking that the noise would annoy shoppers. The Tiedtke brothers, on the other hand, thought their customers would enjoy all the commotion, and their hunch proved right: shoppers immediately began lining up to buy bags of their Parkwood brand coffee.

The owners, who often wore white coats like the store's clerks and enjoyed mingling with customers, brought in bakers of all nationalities, tapping into Toledo's growing population of immigrants, and had them bake their favorite ethnic breads and pastries. Tiedtke's added a peanut roaster, which whistled loudly when the steam built up, as well as a noisy and aromatic popcorn machine. The smells were pumped onto the sidewalks outside the Summit Street store, helping lure customers inside.

Tiedtke's own brand of coffee was named Parkwood after the street in Toledo's stately Old West End neighborhood, where Charles Tiedtke lived. Whirling fans blew the rich aromas of roasted coffee throughout the store's ductwork, enticing customers on all the building's six floors.

Naturally, the aromas made customers hungry, and the Tiedtke brothers realized that it made sense—and profits—to give people a place to eat. So they opened the first of several restaurants inside the store.

They held special direct sales from railroad cars that would pull up on the tracks behind the store, opening their doors to sell fresh fish, meat and other goods at discount.

The store was innovative in numerous ways, including being the first in Toledo with an escalator—a wooden and noisy one—and it was among the earliest stores to experiment with air-conditioning, pumping cold water through first-floor pipes. It didn't work as hoped, cooling just one small area of the massive building, but it illustrated the Tiedtkes' foresight and willingness to invest in new ideas.

At Christmastime, model trains chugged across miniature landscapes at a dozen tables set up throughout the store. And shoppers always turned out in droves when Tiedtke's held its popular holiday toy sales, with prices as low as eighty-eight cents.

All the buzz about the circus-like atmosphere of Tiedkte's drew visitors from throughout northwest Ohio and southeast Michigan, who made the trip downtown to see—and smell—what everybody was talking about.

Charles, the more conservative of the Tiedtke brothers, once looked down from the second balcony at the hustle and bustle on the first floor and commented to Ernest that it looked like a circus. That gave Ernest, the more creative and daring brother, an idea: to add music that would put customers in a good mood. They started playing songs on a phonograph, but the sound wasn't of high-enough quality, so they installed a pipe organ.

Charles Tiedtke said that when the organ notes began booming through the store, he could see sales pick up and shoppers start smiling.

A Boston reporter once wrote:

> *I never had such an unusual experience as going into this delightful place at holiday time and hearing the beautiful "Adestes Fidelis" booming out of the organ, accompanied by the whistle of the peanut roaster and the crash and grind of the coffee machines. There was caviar on one side of me and ice-cold buttermilk on the other. There was a carnival spirit all over the store, and it was an adventure just to go into the place.*

One employee who worked at Tiedtke's in the Roaring Twenties said the store could sell as much as ten thousand loaves of bread, two and a half tons of peanuts, two tons of candy and ten thousand packs of cigarettes in a single day. The delivery department, with ninety bright-yellow horse-drawn wagons, handled up to 4,300 orders per day.

Decades later, Toledoans fondly recall the unique appeal of Tiedtke's.

"The initial impact was the aromas," said Gordon Ward, a longtime Toledo TV newsman. "The moment you walked into the store, there were these magnificent aromas hitting you. Other stores would try to disguise the smells, but Tiedtke's used them as a sales tool. I didn't even drink coffee, but I always wanted to buy some."

Jim MacDonald, a Toledo native who became a columnist for the *Orlando Star Sentinel*, reminisced about Tiedtke's and its aromas in a 1975 column:

> *As you walked in the front door, you immediately smelled the delicious fragrance of freshly prepared hot dogs and hamburgers coming from the standup food counter. Next came a soft whiff from the tobacco department, where cigarettes, cigars and pipes from all parts of the world were sold. Then came the candy department where almost everything sold was made on the premises. You could watch as a machine turned out candy kisses. The bakery department was next. All the breads, pies, cakes, cookies and a huge assortment of rolls had been prepared in the store's bakery. There also was a coffee and tea department, where, of course, the coffee was roasted and ground right in front of your eyes. What an aroma!*

The column inspired many transplanted Toledoans to write to the Orlando paper and describe their fondest memories of Tiedtke's.

"I always enjoyed the fresh donuts, the fresh buttered popcorn, and the fresh roasted peanuts. We patronized the florist department quite often for corsages and other flower arrangements, always priced very reasonably. That store was something else," wrote Carwin Elwick of Ocala.

Chester Piasecki of Winter Haven said the horses that pulled Tiedtke's delivery wagons were "beautiful" animals that "could out run Man O' War."

Irene Spaulding of Sebastian, Florida, fondly recalled buying "Swiss cheese on rye at the Buttermilk Bar in the back of the store," and added that "it was tempting to walk along and not steal" olives from the store's barrels.

Many people remember the first floor of Tiedtke's as being more of a carnival than a department store. There were enough sights, sounds and smells to make every visit an adventure. In the produce department, for example, clerks would stand in the aisles and juggle grapefruits or oranges. Salesmen pitched their wares, from candy, baked goods and sausages to exotic fare that included fried rabbit and buffalo meat.

Cheese was one of the store's specialties, with advertisements boasting "nourishing, appealing…cheeses of all nations—108 domestic and 87 imported, representing 18 countries." Among the selections were French Bel Paese, Swiss Sap Sage, Norwegian Gjetest, Canadian Black Diamond, Italian Parmesan and English Cheshire. During the holiday season, the 3,200-pound "Mammoth Wisconsin Medium Sharp Cheddar" wheel was rolled into the store and cut into slices that sold for sixty-nine cents a pound ($4.30 less per pound than in 2014!).

Businessmen used to joke that it was time to "go over to Tiedtke's and smell our lunch!"

Tiedtke's was decades ahead of its time in offering a broad inventory of goods instead of specializing in a few products like most large retail stores. From its initial stock of groceries and dry goods, Tiedtke's added toys, hardware, furniture, mattresses, shoes, suits, hats, lingerie—even wedding dresses.

Etta Hoot, who turned eighty-seven in 2014, bought her white satin wedding dress with a long train at Tiedtke's for fifty dollars in 1947. She displayed it proudly, along with a wedding photo of herself in the dress, at a "Tiedtke's Days" event held in September 2014 at a senior center in South Toledo. "Tiedtke's was just a special place," Hoot said wistfully.

Several hundred people attended the two-day gathering at

Etta Hoot, at a "Tiedtke's Days" event in 2014, displays the wedding dress she bought at Tiedtke's in 1947. *Author's collection.*

the Margaret Hunt Senior Center, reminiscing about the store that closed more than forty-one years earlier.

"They had circus [funhouse] mirrors in the back hallway," recalled Kathy Jennings. "It was just a treat going there. There were places for snacks throughout the store. So many good things. Why can't they make a store like that now?"

Marti Adams got a job working at Tiedtke's "scramble table," a large display stocked with cheap goods that caused shoppers to "scramble" for bargains like a shoehorn, a sugar scoop or a can opener for just a nickel. "It was my first job—and my favorite job," recalled Adams, who went on to become a nurse.

The store was constantly adding innovations. In 1951, Tiedtke's opened a fish counter, where live lobsters and crabs scuttled across the bottoms of saltwater tanks. One half of the fish storage room featured frozen fish kept at a zero-degree temperature, and the other half had fresh fish at thirty-five degrees, with most of the fish hauled in by the company's boats on Lake Erie. "It was a real treat to be able to see so many large fish in the iced-down cases, most of them whole, and complete with heads and tails," said Ray Lewis of Toledo.

In 1961, Tiedtke's celebrated a "Giant Birthday Sale" with all the hype and hoopla the store was known for. In addition to offering "free gifts for everyone," including puzzles, balloons and slices of cake, the store brought in a literal giant—seven-foot, four-inch-tall Jakob Nacken of Germany, who was billed as "the World's Tallest Man."

Store prices were always kept low, appealing to Toledo's largely blue-collar, middle-class population. "Tiedtke's Bargain Days" ads from the 1950s, for example, featured shoes priced as low as $1.99, a new suit for $29.00, a tie for $1.00, jeans for $1.99 and baby clothes for $0.88.

"The middle-class and poor person could always shop here more easily than the large malls. The merchandise is good, the prices are reasonable and the bus lines to come down here are easy to get to," said Toledoan Helen Coder. Before cultural changes shifted the December advertising campaigns from "Christmas" to "holiday" sales, Tiedtke's proclaimed overtly religious messages in its advertisements. On December 24, 1958, for example, the *Blade* featured a Tiedtke's ad with several pairs of praying hands, a stained-glass window and these lines from Dutch folk song:

We gather together to ask the Lord's blessing.
He chastens and hastens His will to make known;

When Tiedtke's held a "Giant Birthday Sale" in 1961, the store brought in a real giant—seven-foot, four-inch Jakob Nacken of Germany. *Toledo–Lucas County Public Library.*

The wicked oppressing now cease from distressing;
Sing praises to His name; He forgets not His own.
Tiedtke's
Merry Christmas—1958.

The Tiedtke brothers treated employees like family, and there were a number of reports of the owners quietly paying their workers' doctor bills and even paying off the mortgages of employees experiencing financial problems. The only caveat was that the workers were asked not to tell anyone.

Decades after the store closed, former workers continued to hold annual picnics and gather periodically for Tiedtke's Old Timers Club events.

"It's hard for anyone to imagine how much fun it was to work there," Helen Keene told a reporter in 1995. She was seventeen when she was hired to run the coffee-roasting machine, and she worked six days a week for a sixteen-dollar paycheck.

Tiedtke's was also generous to underprivileged children in the community, inviting orphans from St. Anthony Villa and the Miami Children's Home for free shopping sprees every holiday season.

Unlike today's culture, people dressed up to go shopping. They'd call their friends or relatives and arrange to meet at a downtown spot, with Tiedtke's being the most popular meeting place.

"I just enjoy going through the stores down here," said Toledoan Marge Hurst. "It seems that in these new malls all you do is walk and walk until you finally get to the store you want. Their bread and baked goods at Tiedtke's are really great. I always thought this was such a great store just to saunter through."

Charles and Ernest Tiedtke decided to sell their store in 1925, when they were approached by Jerome Kobacker, whose family owned a Columbus department store as well as a downtown Toledo furniture store. The Tiedtkes felt it was a good time to step away from the business into which they had poured their time and energy for more than thirty years. Their decision was made easier by their trust in Kobacker, who said there was no need to make major changes and promised to carry on the Tiedtke's traditions.

Kobacker and his son, Marvin, ran the store from 1925 to 1961 and continued featuring such popular Tiedtke's draws as the pipe organ, the holiday cheese wheel and bargain prices.

In 1928, Jerome Kobacker announced that Tiedtke's had acquired two adjoining properties—the Mininger Building and the H.M.&R. Building—adding thirty-six thousand square feet of space and sixty feet of frontage along Summit Street extending to the corner of Adams Street.

In 1955, Kobacker opened a Tiedtke's annex, selling furniture and appliances, directly across the street from the main store, on the northwest corner of Summit and Adams Streets—adjacent to Trinity Episcopal Church in the former Fair Store. Company officials said it housed the largest home furnishings display in Toledo. The grand opening featured a ribbon-cutting

The Tiedtke's store can be seen in this aerial photo, just to the right of the large parking lot along the Maumee River. *Toledo–Lucas County Public Library*.

ceremony hosted by Gloria Maxwell, Miss Toledo of 1955, and a drawing for $2,500 in household furnishing and appliances.

The Tiedtke's story took a dramatic turn in 1961 when Kobacker Stores sold the landmark Toledo store for $8 million to Federal's Inc., a Detroit-based chain of fifty-three stores. At the time of the sale, Tiedtke's was still thriving in its downtown location, but imminent change was looming in the retail world. Air-conditioned malls had been popping up in the suburbs, catering to the city's changing demographics, and Federal's appointee as Tiedtke's president, Douglas Emmons, vowed to change with the times. He told a reporter soon after the purchase that Tiedtke's would "get more of the retail department look, rather than the glorified Joe's bargain store."

Federal's opened a Tiedtke's branch store in 1969 at Greenwood Mall, at the corner of Lewis Avenue and Alexis Road, and Emmons was delighted to overhear shoppers say that the new outlet "didn't seem like a Tiedtke's store."

"That's what I want to hear," Emmons boasted to a reporter.

That same year, Federal's invested $500,000 in the downtown flagship store, relocating nearly every department, adding carpeting and modern fixtures, closing the fourth floor and eliminating 70 percent of the grocery operation including meats, fruits, vegetables and canned goods. Grocery employees were offered jobs in other departments. The newly consolidated department sold beer and wine, cold cuts, cheese and snack foods. The changes left downtown Toledo without a complete grocery store for the first time in the city's history.

Marvin Kobacker, who had been associated with Tiedtke's for more than forty-four years, said customer traffic "dropped considerably after those changes" and never picked up again.

In February 1972, the Tiedtke's annex was closed, and the furniture and appliances departments were moved back into the main store. Six months later, Federal's parent company, Davidson Brothers, filed a petition for reorganization under federal bankruptcy law and, on August 29, 1972, announced that it was closing the main Tiedtke's store downtown.

The chain's management said Tiedtke's was one of its "marginal operations in three communities which have never played a major role in our overall business."

About 280 full-time and part-time downtown store workers were called into a noon meeting on Wednesday, August 30, and informed that the store's last day of operation would be on Saturday, September 2, just three days away. Many of the workers had already learned of the closing unofficially at a retirement party for the store's general manager the night before.

"People are really going to miss this store when it's gone," lamented Dolores Laubenz, a clerk for twelve years, to a *Blade* reporter. "When you were a kid, it was a big thing to come down to Tiedtke's."

Marvin Kobacker, who was president of Tiedtke's from 1952 until the sale to Federal's in 1961, continued to work in a third-floor office at the downtown building and was teary-eyed during an interview the day the closing was announced. "It was no great shock," he told the *Blade*, "but that still doesn't make it much easier to take."

Thirteen years earlier, Kobacker said, he purchased property to build a Tiedtke's store at the planned Franklin Park Shopping Center in West Toledo, but the expansion plan was overruled by other family members. The decision not to open a store at the suburban shopping center set the scene for Tiedtke's sale to Federal's and, ultimately, for the demise of the downtown store, Kobacker opined.

Burt Silverman, vice-president of the Downtown Toledo Associates, called the closing "a terrible blow to downtown area retailing and to the downtown itself. Tiedtke's was a strong magnet to draw people into the downtown area, and it was a unique store for many years. Certainly some of the people who came downtown because of it will no longer come downtown."

The last big sale at Tiedtke's 408 Summit Street store was held on February 28, 1973, when 150 bargain hunters attended an auction at which Tiedtke's signs, shelves, racks, bakery equipment, tables, desks and more than ten thousand other separate items were sold in 1,500 lots.

A week later, Federal's announced that it was also closing the Tiedtke's store at Greenwood Mall.

In September 1974, a demolition company was razing Tiedtke's six-story annex when debris smashed through the roof of the 111-year-old Trinity Episcopal Church next door, causing several thousand dollars' worth of damage that was later compounded by water damage. Several large windows also were damaged, church officials said. The annex's demolition continued, but the process took an unusually long time because wrecking crews took apart the building's east wall, which bordered Trinity, "brick by brick." Today, an elevated, open-air Trinity Plaza stands on the site of the former Tiedtke's annex.

The landmark Summit Street department store was sold to the City of Toledo and scheduled for demolition, which began in the spring of 1975. On May 7, Robert Hailey, owner of Nashville-based International Demolition & Salvage, Inc., saw what he thought was dust coming from the fourth floor on the building's waterfront side. It turned out to be smoke. He called the fire department, which dispatched a pumper crew at 7:14 p.m.

The first crew to arrive initially saw no signs of fire, but "in a matter of minutes they had a real fire on their hands," fire chief Eulan Tucker said.

Sheets of flame quickly engulfed the seven-story building, and more than one hundred firefighters battled the inferno that raged for more than five hours. In all, the fire department dispatched ten pumpers, seven ladder trucks, a life squad and a rescue squad as the spectacular fire not only destroyed Tiedtke's but also sent burning embers airborne, drifting onto the roofs of the nearby Lion Store Annex and the Edward Lamb Building, where they were extinguished by firemen. Drifting embers also burned a tarpaulin covering the hole in the roof of Trinity Church that was caused by the demolition of Tiedtke's annex.

At the same time, emergency crews had to deal with angry and unruly crowds, who began throwing stones at firefighters after police forced them away from the fire. When police put up barricades to block off downtown intersections, some motorists drove over curbs to get closer to the fire.

Crowds turned out to watch as flames engulfed the seven-story Tiedtke's building on May 7, 1975. *Toledo–Lucas County Public Library.*

Seven firefighters were treated for smoke inhalation at St. Vincent Hospital. Fire officials could not determine the cause of the fire, but Chief Tucker initially called it "suspicious."

"I stood and cried when I watched it burn," said Helen Keene, the former coffee roaster. "It was a one-of-a-kind place that can never be replaced."

Gordon Ward, the Toledo newscaster, said the fire marked the end of an era. He said he had tears in his eyes as he watched the flames destroy the legendary store. "It went out big," he said. "That was the last huge crowd Tiedtke's would ever draw, watching 408 Summit Street disappear beneath a curtain of flames."

2
LAMSON'S

BUSINESS BY THE GOLDEN RULE

In 1870, during what Mark Twain tagged America's "Gilded Age," Toledo was a booming commercial center and growing rapidly. Waves of newcomers were arriving from the east by train, boat and wagon to begin new lives in Ohio. Between 1870 and 1890, Toledo's population grew from 31,584 to 81,434—an increase of more than 260 percent.

The surging population brought many entrepreneurs to the port city who envisioned Toledo as a land of opportunity. Among those who moved west with dreams of making their fortunes were three New York brothers, Julius G. Lamson (b. 1853), C. Edgar B. Lamson (b. 1854) and John D.R. Lamson (b. 1859).

C.E.B. Lamson was the first to leave the family's hometown of Elbridge, in the Finger Lakes Region of upstate New York, to settle in Toledo—where some of his maternal relatives lived. He arrived in the spring of 1872 and landed a job at the Bailey Brothers drugstore on the corner of Monroe and Summit Streets.

On October 6 the next year, his elder brother Julius left Elbridge and also headed for Toledo, where he found work clerking at a dry goods store, Trepanier and Cooper. His goal at the time, according to a 1928 profile, was to "locate in a good community and to make such a place for himself as would entitle him to self-respect and the respect of his neighbors. He succeeded in both enterprises."

In 1881, nine years after arriving in Toledo, C.E.B. moved south to Columbus, Ohio, where he worked as a cashier at a railroad company. About

Lamson Brothers, founded in 1885, moved into this $2.75 million, state-of-the-art department store on Jefferson Avenue and Huron Street in 1928. *Toledo–Lucas County Public Library*.

the same time, Julius Lamson wrote to his younger brother John in Syracuse, New York, proposing that he join him in Toledo and that together they would open a dry goods store. Julius planned to include C.E.B. eventually, once the business was big enough to support all three brothers.

To finance the business, Julius turned to his father-in-law, Doria Tracy, a Toledo real-estate tycoon, who offered to provide the capital needed to get the business started.

John soon joined Julius in Toledo, and the brothers opened their Lamson Brothers Company dry goods store on October 6, 1885, in a modest storefront at 319 Summit Street that was only twenty feet wide and eighty feet deep.

A few days before opening, the brothers bought a newspaper ad two columns wide and four inches deep:

Lamson Brothers
will open their new
DRY GOODS HOUSE
to the trade
Tuesday morning, Oct. 6,
at 9 o'clock
with a stock of first-class dry
goods, all new, bought for cash,
and to be sold for cash.
One Price to All.
LAMSON BROTHERS

The claim of "One Price to All" was significant because it marked a new way of doing business in 1885. Previously, people were used to haggling over retail prices, but Lamson's put an end to that practice, and it caught on with other stores. They pledged that Lamson Brothers would provide dependable service, truthful advertising, good merchandise and fair dealing. The promise of honesty and fairness was summed up in one of the store's foundational slogans: "If you see it in our ad, it is so."

Julius had gone to New York to stock the store with dry goods, spending about $10,000—the equivalent of $250,000 today. Sales on the first day the store opened tallied $167.45.

Within eighteen months, their business had grown to the point where they expanded the building back to the alley behind Summit Street and started using the basement and second floor—doubling their display space.

Business continued to bloom, and in April 1889, as the Lamson brothers were looking to expand further, Julius heard that some unidentified businessmen were looking to purchase the store next to them, the S.H. Frank Co., at 333–335 Summit. He quickly called the owner, S.H. Frank, and told him, "Don't do anything until I see you." Frank met with Julius and said the option to buy the building expired at nine o'clock the next morning. At five minutes after nine, the businessmen had not shown up, and the Lamsons bought the building.

In the year after moving to the bigger building, Lamson Brothers generated $325,000 in sales.

In 1890, C.E.B. moved back to Toledo from Columbus and joined the family business. The trio soon made enough profit to pay Doria Tracy back for his investment, becoming sole proprietors of Lamson's.

Lamson's bought a battery-powered delivery truck in 1899, which is widely believed to have been the first horseless carriage that traveled Toledo's streets.

On February 1, 1905, the Lamson Brothers Company was officially incorporated, with a capital stock of $400,000. Julius was company president, John D.R. was vice-president and C.E.B. was secretary and treasurer.

The store's growth continued, quite literally, over the next few years as the Lamsons acquired more properties along Summit Street, razing several adjacent buildings and erecting a five-story addition. In 1910, they acquired the Lasalle & Koch's building, a five-story department store at the corner of Adams and Summit Streets, giving them 160 feet of frontage on the city's main retail center, Summit Street, with entrances on both Summit and Adams.

The company's mail-order business also was thriving. In 1914, the Lamsons' noted that they were shipping products to customers as far away as Point Barrow, Alaska, and Punta Arenas, Chile, in South America. They did business "wherever the English language is spoken and American periodicals are taken." Lamson's mail-order department was staffed by thirty-seven employees, and it spent more than $122,000 on stamps, money orders and fees that year.

John D.R. Lamson, meanwhile, had also become a successful inventor, obtaining patents for such devices as a hook-and-eye fastener, a toy savings bank, a mechanical pencil and a "vehicle tractor." When John died in 1915 at age fifty-six, leaving a wife and four children, his position in the family corporation was assumed by Julius's son-in-law, Sydney Vinnedge.

By 1916, the store was hemmed in at its Summit Street location, and the owners began scouting downtown for a suitable site. After an extensive study, Lamson Brothers made the bold move of building at the northeast corner of Jefferson Avenue and Huron Street, four blocks west of Summit Street on the site of the former Little Spitzer Building. Lamson's leased the property for ninety-nine years with an option to buy.

Ground was broken on the five-story, $2.75 million building on April 12, 1928, with Julius Lamson turning over the ceremonial first spade of dirt—getting a helping hand from his five-year-old grandson, Jules Vinnedge (who eventually would succeed him as president of the Lamson Brothers).

H.J. Spieker Co., general contractor, completed construction in seven months, lauded in the media as record time for such a large project, and more than 70 percent of all building materials were Toledo products or locally supplied. The grand opening was set for November 13, 1928, with shoppers strolling to music provided by Sydney's Orchestra.

"With brief and simple ceremonies Lamson's beautiful and modern store…was dedicated to the service of Toledoans and thrown open for public inspection at noon Tuesday," the *Blade* reported.

> *President Julius G. Lamson, one of the founders of this institution more than 43 years ago and still its directing head, renewed his pledge of faith in Toledo and service to its citizens in a short talk, the sincerity of which deeply affected his audience. Continuation of his policies of honesty and dependability, in strict conformity with the Golden Rule, which has been his motto through life, were promised by President Lamson in the operation of this greatly enlarged enterprise, just as fully as when the store was first opened in 319 Summit St. more than two-score years ago with less than a dozen employees.*

The new building had 200 feet of frontage on Huron Street and 128 feet on Jefferson, with merchandise displayed on four floors of 38,000 square feet each and the fifth floor for offices and a stock room. The façade of the Italian Renaissance design was made of 1,240 tons of Indiana Oolithic limestone, and 17 tons of Cold Spring rainbow granite from Minnesota were used for the base. More than 465 tons of steel were used in its framework.

The new Lamson Brothers store was regarded as a marvel for its time. The foundation was designed to accommodate two more floors if the owners later decided to add on.

Six new De Luxe trucks, each with a capacity of one ton, could drive down a ramp from Erie Street into the basement, where they would be loaded with packages sent down on spiral chutes of steel and then sorted by destination. On the roof were two water tanks, each with a nine-thousand-gallon capacity, feeding an automatic sprinkler system through concealed piping.

The store featured broad aisles, elegant Italian-style columns on the main floor and six elevators that could carry twenty-five people at a time at a speed of six feet per second—going from basement to the top floor in nineteen seconds. Two freight elevators could carry more than two tons each. The *Blade* noted the building's "marvelous ventilating plant" in which "both warm air and cold air is constantly introduced into the building after it has been washed. It passes through a curtain of oil. The ventilation represents the latest inventions in that kind of equipment."

Heat was provided from a central plant, with no coal or fuel inside the department store. The temperature was kept at a comfortable seventy degrees year-round. More than thirty-six miles of electric wire were used to supply 200,000 candlepower of lighting, enough to provide power for the village of Perrysburg at the time.

Merchandise "from the far corners of the world" was put on display in departments that included fur, furniture, lingerie, men's clothing, luggage, watch repair, a tearoom, paint, wallpaper and dry cleaning. The store also featured a bakery, a photographic studio and a beauty parlor with twenty-five operators and employees. There would be no "bargain tables" on the four main retail floors but only in the basement, store officials announced. Lamson's added that it would continue its policy of selling "no seconds or irregulars" anywhere in the building.

Flanking the three arched entrances were pairs of medallions bearing the insignia of ancient guilds from Florence, Italy—butchers and tanners, dressers and dyers, cloth manufacturers, silk manufacturers, mercers and linen drapers and furriers—symbolizing integrity, quality and craftsmanship.

Less than two years after the new store opened, Julius Lamson stepped down as president and was succeeded by his son-in-law, Sydney Vinnedge. (C.E.B. Lamson had already retired.)

In September, 1935, the *Toledo News-Bee* announced in a headline that "Lamson Bros. Will Celebrate Golden Jubilee With Greatest Sale in History of Company." Julius Lamson, at age eighty-three, was honored at a special anniversary dinner attended by six hundred employees.

"We have no boast. Business has just come along," he said at the gala. "We have gone through depressions but in all the fifty years we have never missed a payroll. Sometimes we have had to scrape the bottom of the till but we got it."

Julius Lamson was honored for his civic leadership, including his support of the Young Men's Christian Association, the Young Women's Christian Association, his honorary presidency of the Toledo Council of Churches, his leadership in the Retail Merchants' Board and his longtime membership at Ashland Avenue Baptist Church.

His religious beliefs led to Lamson's policy of being closed on Sundays to observe the biblical fourth commandment: "Thou shalt keep holy the Lord's day." The store's large display windows were always draped on Saturday evening and stayed that way until Monday morning. Lamson's never advertised on Sundays.

After Julius retired as president, he remained active in the store's leadership as chairman of the board, a post he held until his death in 1942, just two days after turning eighty-nine.

Baby furnishing displayed in a Lamson's store window. To observe the Sabbath, the store covered all its windows on Sundays. *Toledo–Lucas County Public Library.*

Lamson's was the first of the large downtown Toledo department stores to open branches in the suburbs. In July 1943, it opened a relatively small store in the location of a former department store at Conant and East Wayne Streets in Maumee, on Toledo's southern border.

In November 1951, Lamson's opened a much larger branch with great fanfare in the Colony district, remodeling a twenty-thousand-square-foot building on Central Avenue and Monroe Street, with parking for two thousand cars. The new building was considered "ultra modern" by the media, which noted its air conditioning, wide aisles and "many of the latest features in merchandising."

A crowd estimated at thirty thousand attended the grand opening, which featured strolling musicians, gifts for children, flowers for women and speeches by Lamson's new president, Fern Kettel; Toledo mayor Ollie Czelusta; and Walter Lathrop, owner of the construction firm that built the new store.

Kettel noted "the need for more shopping centers in suburban areas that include parking facilities for shoppers," an observation that proved prophetic for the rise of suburban malls and the eventual demise of downtown retail.

On March 11, 1955, Lamson's opened another large branch store, at the intersection of the Anthony Wayne Trail and Detroit Avenue. The forty-thousand-square-foot facility was the first of twenty-five stores scheduled to open at Parkway Plaza shopping center. Lamson's newest branch featured "modern, open-back type" display windows, "which permit the customer to view the interior of the store as well as the featured merchandise," a *Toledo Times* reporter noted, adding that "the main floor has been carefully laid out for easy, convenient shopping. By coordinating selling areas, it is possible for the customer to purchase an entire wardrobe with a minimum of steps."

Sixteen years later, Lamson's renewed its commitment to the suburbs by opening a ninety-thousand-square-foot store at the new Franklin Park Mall on July 20, 1971, joining J.C. Penney and J.L. Hudson as anchor stores at the elegant and modern West Toledo mall. Developer James Rouse called it "a marketplace and shopping atmosphere second to none in America."

The next year, Lamson's opened yet another branch, this one an 82,000-square-foot facility at a new shopping center in South Toledo, the 950,000-square-foot Southwyck Mall.

The booming commercial centers in the city suburbs took a toll on downtown retail. Jules Vinnedge, Julius Lamson's grandson and president of the company since 1961, announced on April 2, 1974, that the company would close its downtown store in two weeks. The branches at Parkway Plaza, Franklin Park and Southwyck would stay open, he said. The closure resulted

The former Lamson's store was renamed One Lake Erie Center in 1978, housing offices and a charter school. *Author's collection.*

from a fifteen-year decline in downtown business, Vinnedge said. "People do not come downtown anymore. You've got to go where they are," he said.

Two months later, Lamson's sold its Franklin Park store to Jacobson's, a luxury chain headquartered in Jackson, Michigan.

In April 1976, Lamson's filed for bankruptcy protection, and in September of that year, the company was purchased by Schottenstein Stores Corporation of Columbus. The new owners renamed the Parkway Plaza store Lamson's Value City and announced it would close the Southwyck store by October 31.

Southwyck Mall, which once boasted a lineup of 103 stores, struggled for years and closed in June 2008. The sprawling edifice was demolished the following year and today is a vacant stretch of weeds, concrete and blacktop. The City of Toledo bought the property in 2014 with vague plans of resurrecting it. Lamson's Value City store at Parkway Plaza closed in 2008, and the building has been bulldozed. Jacobson's declared bankruptcy in 2002, and its store at Franklin Park Mall was demolished two years later, making way for a new wing with a movie complex and a Dick's Sporting Goods store.

The only Lamson's landmark building still in existence is its downtown flagship store, which was renamed One Lake Erie Center in 1978. It now houses a charter school and government offices.

3
LASALLE'S
ELEGANCE IN RETAIL

Like Tiedtke's and Lamson's, Lasalle's was a landmark downtown department store for generations. With upscale products and imaginative marketing, it was a favorite among Toledo-area shoppers from the end of the Civil War until the 1980s, when it was renamed Macy's by its longtime corporate owners.

The original dry goods store was founded by Jacob Lasalle, an emigrant from Prussia, who had fought for the Union in the Civil War, joining a regiment of German-born Jews in the Eighty-second Regiment of the Illinois Volunteer Infantry.

After settling in Toledo, Lasalle partnered with Joseph Epstein to found the Lasalle & Epstein dry goods store at 51 Summit Street, opening on September 14, 1865.

In 1881, the partners merged with another successful dry goods company owned by Joseph Koch (pronounced "Cook"), a German immigrant, and Alies S. Cohen. Cohen left three years later to pursue other business interests, and the company was renamed Lasalle & Koch, a name that became a familiar, influential force in Toledo's retail scene.

Lasalle and Koch quickly outgrew their five-story building on Summit Street in Toledo's downtown retail district and in 1890 made what they described as "a daring move" by relocating several blocks away to a brick-and-stone six-story building on Jefferson Avenue and Superior Street. "This was far from the popular shopping district and many timid souls predicted disaster," the company stated in an ad. "But Toledo continued to grow, and Lasalle & Koch's with it."

The store continued to do brisk business selling fabrics, carpets, furniture, shoes and home furnishings, among other items, and the owners outgrew their facility. In both 1906 and 1908, they added more frontage along Superior Street, expanding to 140,000 square feet of floor space.

When Joseph Koch died unexpectedly in 1904, at age fifty-four, he was succeeded by his son, Alfred B. Koch, who gave up his studies at the University of Michigan to return to Toledo and help run the business. He was named general manager, and under his leadership, Lasalle & Koch made another bold move, one that would shake up the downtown shopping district for decades. In August 1916, Koch announced that Lasalle & Koch Co. was planning to build "a splendid edifice" eight stories high with nearly 400,000 square feet of space in a downtown area that was not known for retail, the corner of Adams and Huron Streets.

The new store would be built at 513 Adams, the site of the National Union Building that had been erected in 1892 as the headquarters of National Union insurance company, which specialized in coverage for fraternal organizations. The Romanesque and Gothic building featured eighty offices and a large auditorium where Toledoans got their first glimpse of Thomas Edison's Kinetescope, the precursor of motion picture projectors. It was the largest Toledo building to be demolished when it was razed in 1916. The property also marked the boundary lines between two rival pioneer villages, Port Lawrence and Vistula, whose union in 1833 led to the 1837 incorporation of the city of Toledo.

Construction of the new Lasalle & Koch store was financed by Edward Drummond Libbey, father of Toledo's glass industry, and the building was designed by Starrett and Van Vleck, the prominent New York architectural firm whose credits include Lord and Taylor on Fifth Avenue and Saks Fifth Avenue in Manhattan. "The new store will be as modern, as up-to-date and as artistic as money can make it," Koch said in announcing the project.

Construction took fourteen months, and as the grand opening approached, Lasalle & Koch piqued Toledoans' interest with a series of flowery newspaper ads describing the company's vision for the new flagship store. "After all the long days and nights—after all the effort of hand and heart and brain—next Tuesday morning we shall dedicate to your use our new home. Imagination wove a canvas and painted a picture, an ideal. It is now about to face the reality—the result of its handicraft—the dream-of-dreams will have come true. The splendid edifice and all that it contains will be ready to serve you," the first ad said in part.

When the Lasalle & Koch department store opened on Adams Street in 1917, it declared the start of "The New Era" for Toledo and vicinity. *Toledo–Lucas County Public Library.*

A subsequent ad, titled "The New Era," loftily proclaimed: "With the opening of our doors in this splendid edifice comes 'The New Era'—not to us alone, nor to our customers, but to the whole of Toledo and vicinity. The standard of living has been changed for every family that comes within its sphere of influence… Our beautiful store in its beauty and the splendid things it contains has made Toledo different for you for all times hereafter. It is 'The New Era.'"

When the doors opened on Tuesday, November 13, 1917, an estimated ninety thousand people entered through the arched doorways to marvel at Toledo's new monument to retail. The main floor featured a series of polished granite columns supporting the majestic twenty-nine-foot ceiling, rows of mahogany display cases, extra-wide aisles, travertine limestone floors and a curved wall with a bank of six elevators whose doors were made of mahogany and bronze.

One reporter described the interior as "cathedral-like," and the *Blade* gushed that Lasalle & Koch "singled out this city as enterprising enough and 'metropolitan' enough to deserve and to vindicate the finest store in America." The two-story Corinthian-style colonnade of the top floors echoed the ground-floor exterior, and a projecting cornice overhung the sidewalks, protecting shoppers from the rain.

The building connected to the Spitzer Arcade, another downtown landmark, and the indoor walking space was lauded, among other places, in a 1917 edition of *The Corset and Underwear Review*: "In inclement weather a person can enter the Spitzer Building on Huron Street [and walk] through the office building and department store to Adams Street."

Merchandise that was sold on the main floor included books, candy, stationery, men's clothing, handbags, hosiery, jewelry and a flower shop. The next six floors featured merchandise and services, including a beauty salon and photo studio, beachwear, luggage, housewares and toys. The eighth floor comprised an auditorium and restaurants.

The new store was so successful that, in just one month, its sales were equal to those of an entire year at its previous location. Bruce Allen Kopytek, in his book *Toledo's Three Ls: Lamson's, the Lion Store, and Lasalle's*, observed that with the 1917 opening of the new Lasalle & Koch store, the "retail map of Toledo was forever changed," shifting away from Summit Street and transforming the corner of Adams and Huron into what became known as "the Hub of Toledo."

The exterior of Lasalle's in 2015 looks much like it did when it opened in 1917. The interior has been converted into apartments. *Author's collection.*

It didn't take long for other large retailers to enter the picture. In 1923, just five years after the new Lasalle's opened, R.H. Macy and Company bought "an interest" in the store as the New York retail giant began building a nationwide chain. Control of the Toledo store would remain with Alfred Koch, Macy's asserted.

Almost ten years to the day that the Lasalle & Koch flagship store opened, the company held a grand opening for three news floors that added seventy-five thousand square feet of space. The eighth floor's auditorium and restaurants were completely redone. One of the restaurants, the elegant French Room, was described by the *Blade* as "a masterpiece of artistry…The color combinations and blending of the walls, the carpeting, the chairs and tables themselves and the indirect lighting effects produce an amazing effect, the first glimpse of which brings a gasp of astonishment and admiration."

Lasalle & Koch was known for creative marketing and lavish events, notably its children's style shows. In January 1922, Julia Coburn, the store's advertising manager, wrote a column for the *Dry Goods Economist*, a national publication, extolling the success of its children's fashion shows held in the store's auditorium:

> *That a style revue need not be just the usual fashion parade has been successfully proved by the Lasalle & Koch Co., Toledo, Ohio in the semi-annual children's style revues which it has presented during the last few years. Last spring, when the affair came very soon after President* [Warren G.] *Harding's inauguration, a miniature White House was used on the stage as a background, and the authentic Harding Blue was introduced in youthful attire by the Harding Blue Kiddies.*
>
> *For the fall revue last year, the idea of art in children's dress was taken as a theme and a perfect replica of the Art Museum, Toledo's most beloved and representative building, complete even to its pillars, its broad marble steps and the hospitable lighting of its cornice, greeting the audience of 3,000 or more which gathered in Lasalle & Koch's auditorium Saturday afternoon, Nov. 19, to see the much-heralded revue.*

One of the store's notable employees was Betty Warren, the future wife of President Gerald Ford. She grew up in Grand Rapids, Michigan, and, after moving to the Toledo suburb of Maumee, worked as a model at Lasalle's in the 1940s.

The Lasalle & Koch Co. was among the first Toledo department stores to open branches after World War II. In fact, it purchased a building on Main Street in Bowling Green, Ohio, in 1944, before the war ended. Over the next decade, Lasalle's added branches in the northwest Ohio cities of Tiffin, Findlay and Sandusky.

In 1962, Lasalle's opened the first suburban Toledo branch at Westgate Village Shopping Center, an ambitious outdoor mall at the corner of Secor Road and Central Avenue, seven miles from downtown. The new building featured 152,000 square feet of space and was designed by noted San Francisco architect John Savage Bolles, who also designed Candlestick Park, former home of the San Francisco Giants baseball team. "Now you can have Lasalle's any way you like us…Downtown or Suburban Style," the company said in an advertisement.

A second suburban Lasalle's store opened at Woodville Mall in the suburb of Northwood in August 1969, and the company opened its biggest suburban branch, a 162,000-square-foot facility, at North Towne Square Mall in 1980.

Woodville Mall never achieved the level of success of the other suburban malls, and after initial success, North Towne also began to struggle as Franklin Park Mall became the dominant suburban shopping center.

Macy's, which had been controlling Lasalle's from behind the scenes for decades, stepped to the forefront and put its name on the company's Adams Street and Westgate stores in 1981.

In January 1984, Macy's closed the once-majestic downtown department store, and it wasn't long before the branch stores in Bowling Green, Tiffin and Sandusky were also shuttered.

In 1985, Macy's sold its Westgate Village and Findlay stores to the Elder-Beerman Stores Corporation, a department store chain based in Dayton, Ohio. Elder-Beerman continues to operate the former Lasalle's store at Westgate Village.

Former employees held a reunion in October 1989 and reminisced about the good old days. Among the 250 former employees who attended was Margaret Littleton, who retired in 1975 after twenty-eight years in the men's department. "I enjoyed every minute of it. It was a great store," she told the *Blade*.

The downtown flagship store sat vacant for years before the developers obtained a $12 million tax break in 1997 and converted the facility into a 131-unit apartment building. That renovation has been a resounding success, with occupancy rates averaging well over 90 percent. Residents love the building but are not thrilled with the neighborhood. "As soon as we moved in, we realized there pretty much was no downtown action," one apartment resident told the *Blade* in 2008. "We didn't have any problems or break-ins, but it was just super boring. There was just more to do in the suburbs."

4
LION STORE

LOCAL LOYALTY

Generations of Toledoans remember climbing atop a pair of cast-iron lions that had guarded the entrance to a downtown Toledo department store for more than one hundred years. It all started in 1857, when Frederick K. Eaton founded what eventually would become the Lion Store.

Born in 1836 and raised on a farm in Sutton, New Hampshire, Eaton was one of nine children. Two of his elder brothers went to Dartmouth College and became high-ranking Union officers, including John, who was later appointed brigadier general by President Ulysses S. Grant.

For Frederick, however, "circumstances compelled him to forego the advantages of a collegiate education, which to most aspiring youth is an object of worth ambition; but it does not always afford the best training for business success," wrote Clark Waggoner in his 1888 book *History of the City of Toledo and Lucas County, Ohio*. Eaton worked as a retail clerk in New Hampshire "only long enough to get a little means wherewith to establish business for himself," according to Waggoner. He earned $50 in his first year, $75 the next and $100 the following year. By then, he was "so well up in proficiency and reputation" that he was paid $300 the next year by a larger dry goods store.

He moved to Toledo in August 1857, where his nephew, John Eaton Jr., was superintendent of the Toledo city schools.

In September 1856, when he was twenty-one years old, Frederick partnered with John to open the Frederick Eaton & Co. dry goods store at 115 Summit Street. Their timing was not the greatest. "The year

This rooftop view shows the Lion Store complex on St. Clair Street in the 1920s. Trinity Episcopal Church is visible across Adams Street. *Toledo–Lucas County Public Library.*

of commencement was inauspicious, for it was the year of 'The Great Panic of '57,' which was precipitated by the failure of the Ohio Trust Company in October, and was widespread and disastrous in its results," Waggoner wrote.

Frederick Eaton slept on the store's counters at night "as a substitute for insurance policies and burglar-proof safes," and his company was able to pull through the panic. First-year sales totaled $15,000 and soon began a steady climb.

The next year, the company moved to a slightly larger building at 79 Summit and moved again in 1863 to a building at the corner of Summit Street and Madison Avenue. Sometime in the early 1860s, Eaton commissioned the casting of the two one-thousand-pound lions.

In 1866, the department store moved to 325 Summit, on a stretch known as "Toledo's Grand Promenade," where the statues guarded both sides of the store's main entrance. The store moved several times during those early years, and so did the lions. Children were especially drawn to the fierce-looking felines, and family trips downtown were not considered complete until the youngsters had taken their turn sitting atop the iron animals.

One of the two cast-iron lions that "guarded" the entrance to the Lion Store for more than a century. *Toledo–Lucas County Public Library*.

In 1872, the company's store was destroyed by fire, and Eaton built a new four-story building in its place. The fire didn't slow down the company's rapid growth, however, with Frederick Eaton & Co. employing two hundred clerks and ringing up $1.25 million in sales in 1872.

In 1885, the company added a new partner, George M. Fisher, who had moved from St. Louis, and the store was renamed Fisher, Eaton & Co. The public, however, was increasingly referring to their business as "the Lion Store," thanks to the popular cast-iron statues.

After Frederick Eaton died on January 2, 1897, Fisher ended up buying out the other partners in 1890. He officially changed the name of the store to match the public's moniker, "the Lion Dry Goods Co." Lion continued to expand, adding a four-story building in 1904 that fronted on St. Clair Street, the busy commercial strip behind the Summit Street building. A tunnel and bridge spanned the alley to connect the two properties.

In 1910, Lion acquired a three-story building on St. Clair and Adams Streets and, soon after, added the Trinity Building on St. Clair Street, for a total of 120,000 square feet across a hodgepodge of connected buildings. The grand opening was heralded in a 1910 newspaper ad headlined "The Story of the Lion Store":

> *Years ago, when the present metropolitan city of Toledo was a thriving village of some twenty odd thousand—there stood on what is now its busiest thoroughfare—a one-story frame building which housed the most elaborate department store of its time.*
>
> *There, hardly a century after the freedom of our country—famous beauties were wont to gather and buy of the treasured finery that graced many a notable gathering during this period.*

The ad said the new building "stands for a new era in department store usefulness" and called it "your grandmother's store—your mother's store—your store—the newer and better Lion Store."

Lion continued to acquire neighboring buildings over the years, including the Toledo News Building, built around 1890 at 330 St. Clair Street, the New Tavern Hotel and the Blade Printing and Paper Co., circa 1900.

Lion Store, meanwhile, had been acquired by a New York department store chain, H.B. Claflin Co., which fell into receivership in 1914. After months of court proceedings, Toledo's Lion Store became part of the newly formed Mercantile Stores Co., a New York holding company that operated Lion for the next eighty years.

The downtown store's conglomeration of buildings featured frontage on three major downtown streets—Summit, St. Clair and Adams—and shoppers who traveled from one building to another inevitably had to go up or down ramps or stairs to get to the next floor. Beverly Chandler, a copywriter for Lion Store, recalled having a desk on a ramp between two buildings. "If I wanted to talk to someone at the next desk, I simply gave a little push and my chair rolled down the incline," she said.

Sometimes shoppers even had to walk outside to get to another building. "For a time it was necessary to walk down a few steps to a couple of heavy glass doors that opened onto an often blustery, cold, damp alley," *Blade* reporter John Grigsby once recalled. "The journey required a sharp eye for delivery trucks on the way across the cobblestones to the next building, which was entered through glass doors and up the steps."

He added that there was "a rickety elevator" at the rear of the Summit building "that offered a shaky ride to the upper floors." He also recalled the Coral Room, which for many years was a popular downtown coffee shop on the first floor of the Summit Street building.

"It wasn't the most razzle-dazzle, but people felt a real loyalty to that store," said Toledoan Lois Nelson.

In 1944, as World War II drew to an end, Lion expanded by opening a branch store on Main Street in Bowling Green, about twenty-five miles south of Toledo, where it sold appliances and home furnishings. The next year, it opened a clothing store in the same city.

In November 1950, Lion opened a small branch store in a three-story furniture outlet in Fremont, Ohio, about forty miles southeast of Toledo.

The first suburban Toledo branch was opened at Westgate Village Shopping Center, in West Toledo, in a 100,000-square-foot, two-story building. Westgate was the city's premier mall at the time, and Lion thrived to the point that it added a third floor in 1960, expanding the building to 150,000 square feet, and added yet another 36,000 square feet three years later.

Around the same time, Lion invested half a million dollars in its downtown buildings, making extensive renovations to the aging structures—including the addition of escalators. As Lion was building up its array of stores in Toledo, it closed the branches in Bowling Green and Fremont, citing increased competition and declining sales.

The next expansion was a major one for Lion Store, as the retailer went into partnership with a developer to build Southwyck Mall on Reynolds Road. The new Lion Store, which opened in 1972, covered a sprawling 190,000 square feet, more than twice the size of Lamson's, another Southwyck anchor store. In April 1978, Lion added a second Southwyck store, the 80,000-square-foot Lion for the Home, which was devoted exclusively to items for the home, including furniture, appliances, towels and linens. Lion's $4 million expansion gave the company more than a third of the total retail space at Southwyck.

As the retail centers continued to move to the suburbs, sales in the central business district fell sharply. Just as one-time retail powerhouses Tiedtke's, Lamson's and Lasalle's all closed their downtown stores, Lion eventually shuttered its historic flagship building in 1980. The closing coincided with Lion's opening of a 162,000-square-foot store at North Towne Square, a cavernous facility at Alexis Road and Detroit Avenue along the Michigan border.

In August 1993, Lion opened another branch store, this one a 190,000-square-foot facility at Franklin Park Mall—a mall that quickly became the city's most popular shopping destination. Both the Southwyck and North Towne malls experienced initial success but soon began to struggle mightily. Both sprawling buildings have been closed and razed and are now just vacant, weed-infested lots.

Demolition of the downtown Lion Store began in 1982 and was conducted in phases, ending in 1987. The cast-iron lions were moved to the Toledo Zoo, where they guarded the Carnivore Building from late 1979 until 1982, when they were moved to the Lion Store at Southwyck Mall in 1982. The historic statues were moved to Franklin Park Mall when it opened in 1993.

In 1998, Lion's parent company, Mercantile Stores Co., was purchased by Dillard's Inc., an Arkansas-based chain. Dillard's promised to "tread lightly" on the Lion Store legacy, but it quickly ended one of Lion's most popular events, the quarterly "Moonlight Madness" sales. In 1999, the Lion Store name and logos were replaced by Dillard's marquees at Franklin Park, Southwyck, Westgate and North Towne Square Mall.

The historic Lion Store lions are still on guard, now at the Dillard's department store in Franklin Park Mall. Dillard's acquired Lion Store in 1998. *Author's collection.*

Lion's Westgate store was demolished in 2006, along with Thackeray's Books, Boogie Records and other local favorites, to make room for a Costco members-only warehouse store.

One place where the legendary Lion Store's DNA remains is at the Dillard's department store in Franklin Park Mall. When the Lion Store opened at the mall in 1993, the two cast-iron lions that had once guarded the company's downtown entrance were given a fresh coat of gold paint and lifted by a crane atop two twenty-five-foot-high perches inside the store. Dillard's considered removing the iconic statues when it bought the store in 1998, but the statues' weight made it cost-prohibitive. The famous Toledo lions, and all the memories they inspire, remain on display in the middle of Dillard's.

5
PORTSIDE FESTIVAL MARKETPLACE

HOPE FOR THE FUTURE

In the early 1980s, downtown Toledo was locked in a downward spiral. Two of its landmark department stores had closed their flagship stores forever—first Tiedtke's in 1973 and then Lamson's the next year. The third, Lasalle's, had been transformed into Macy's and was struggling to survive.

"Urban revitalization" had brought the wrecking ball to many historic downtown buildings, razing the skid-row area near Summit and Cherry Streets that had become an eyesore of pawnshops, seedy bars, flophouses and crumbling storefronts. Toledo's woes were part of a nationwide recession in which unemployment reached 10.8 percent and interest rates on thirty-year mortgages topped 16.0 percent. The manufacturing industries were losing to foreign competition, and banks were failing at record rates.

Small wonder, then, in light of such a bleak backdrop, that Toledo's hopes were lifted by the announcement that a $14.5 million shopping center would be built on the downtown riverfront. Portside Festival Marketplace was being developed by James Rouse, a visionary businessman whose credits included numerous downtown retail centers such as Faneuil Hall Marketplace in Boston, South Street Seaport in New York City and Harborplace in Baltimore.

Toledo's new marketplace was envisioned as the "catalyst" for downtown's rebirth, and Rouse asserted that it would have "a transforming impact for Toledo." It had worked in Baltimore, he said, where Harborplace

Portside Festival Marketplace opened in this blue-roofed building in 1984 but closed in 1990. Today, it is the home of the Imagination Station hands-on science museum. *Author's collection.*

gave new life to "an ugly, dirty, filthy waterfront" and helped draw 20 million people downtown in 1982. People "want to see the heart of the city beat again," Rouse said with enthusiasm.

Ground was broken for Portside in December 1982, on almost the spot where the beloved Tiedtke's department store once stood. Beneath the 100,000-square-foot building's bright blue metal roof, the plans called for more than eighty shops and restaurants that would sell flowers, kites, candies, candles, toys, jewelry, ice cream, T-shirts, souvenirs and just about anything a shopper would expect to find in a "festival marketplace."

Willard Scott, the gregarious NBC weatherman, broadcast four live weathercasts from Portside's main stage on Friday, May 18, 1984, the day before the official opening. "This place is really incredible," he said. "Something like this really makes you feel good because you can see the spirit coming back."

The night before, Portside hosted an upscale "Passport to the Arts" party, which the *Blade*'s longtime society columnist Dorothy Rainie hailed as "the largest social gala to ever light up downtown Toledo."

"As the three entrances of Portside were thrown open—promptly at 8 p.m.—what a scene, what a glittering scene!" Rainie gushed.

The Toledo Symphony Brass Quintet performed, hors d'oeuvres and sparkling champagne were served to 2,500 guests and Rainie wrote that it was "such a joy" "to see Toledoans wearing beautiful, long evening gowns and dressy, above-the-ankle cocktail dresses, when their escorts are wearing black-tie."

Before Portside's doors opened for business at noon on Saturday, May 19, 1984, a two-hundred-entry parade, including seven high school marching bands, strode through downtown. A skydiver trailing red, white and blue smoke descended from the clouds, and Ohio governor Richard Celeste joined in the ribbon-cutting ceremony. Portside Festival Marketplace would be the star to light the way to a bright future for downtown Toledo.

It was a distinctive design, with plenty of glass, earth tones and terra cotta topped by the cheery blue roof. Inside were three levels of shops and restaurants as well as merchandise kiosks and a food court. Balconies from all levels overlooked the central atrium and stage, which was splashed with greenery from potted plants and trees. An array of entertainers kept shoppers amused, from clowns and jugglers to brass bands and folk groups. A few years later, Detroit rock icon Mitch Ryder played a New Year's Eve concert at Portside. "We're different from malls," said chief architect Morton Hoppenfeld. "The whole thing was conceived as a setting for life."

Advertisements promised more than just a shopping trip or a meal: "It's enchanting. A delight. An adventure. Magic. Fun. It's unforgettable. And now, at last, you will experience it. Portside Festival Marketplace."

Officials predicted the marketplace would attract five million visitors the first year and generate $13 million to $15 million in business.

Dining establishments included two fine restaurants, Real Seafood and Il Porto, and nearly twenty casual eateries, such as the Great Steak Escape, Afternoon Delight and the Magic Wok—drawing downtown workers planning on a quick and inexpensive lunch.

Shoppers could browse through vinyl records at Abbey Road, sort through the displays at Maumee Wines, pick out a hat at House of Chapeaux, buy a Mud Hens souvenir or treat themselves to dessert at Menke Bakery or Steve's Ice Cream. One of the stores specialized in all things purple. Portside "completely changed the ambiance of downtown," said J. Michael Porter, president of the Toledo Area Chamber of Commerce.

William Brower, a *Blade* columnist, said the opening of Portside Festival Marketplace sparked "a spontaneous swelling of civic pride" and marked "the dawning of a new era in the commercial life of downtown." If Portside didn't reawaken downtown merchandising and entertainment, Brower added, "Toledo is in deep trouble." His words proved all-too prophetic.

Portside drew 4.2 million visitors the first year and rang up $14.8 million in sales. Mayor Doug DeGood said it generated seven hundred to nine hundred jobs.

But within two years, annual attendance plummeted to 2.2 million. Many of the shop and restaurant owners closed up and moved to the suburbs. A number of storefronts were boarded up and stayed that way for embarrassingly long stretches. In March 1986, only fifty-six of the original eighty-one shops remained. Twenty of those sold food, and thirty-six were retail stores—of those, ten were the small, portable kiosks. A meat market, fish market and pastry shop all had closed. Il Porto restaurant was replaced by Louie's Lightning Grill, which gave way two years later to Shooters restaurant and bar, which built an outdoor pool on the waterfront patio.

Rouse said surveys consistently showed that parking—more specifically, the cost of parking, at seventy-five cents for the first half hour—was the biggest complaint from Portside shoppers. "You can't expect people used to parking for free for twenty years [at suburban malls] to get used to paying," one Portside official said.

Other problems cited by Rouse included poor signage pointing people to the marketplace, the slow growth of downtown housing and a lack of other nearby attractions. Winter was an especially slow season, having a bigger impact on attendance than officials had expected.

As financial details later emerged, it was clear that Portside Festival Marketplace was in economic trouble from the start, burdened by a $20 million mortgage at 14 percent interest. Banks, government development agencies and private investors were left holding the bag.

Portside Festival Marketplace closed its doors on September 21, 1990, six years after it was heralded as the crowning jewel of Toledo's new downtown.

A wide range of options was then debated for bringing the abandoned building back to life. Proposals included renaming it "Underground Toledo," with nightlife such as sports bars, comedy clubs and jazz cafés to bring in college students and young adults.

Public hearings were held on ways to save Portside. One frequently voiced idea was to turn it into a casino. One person attending a hearing suggested the building be turned it into "a playground of the future" with waterparks and a computer center. A senior citizen said it was an ideal place for a theater and variety store.

Many of Toledo's homeless people, meanwhile, made use of the empty building by camping out in the tunnels that led to Portside. "It wasn't designed as a hotel, but that's what the former marketplace has become for the hundreds of homeless who have dodged the cold winds over the last few winters by sleeping on its stone floors," the *Blade* noted in 1992.

The building reopened in 1996 as a Toledo branch of the Columbus-based COSI, the Center for Science and Industry. That effort lasted for more than ten years before budget constraints forced it to close on December 31, 2007.

The building reopened on October 10, 2009, as Imagination Station, another science center, but this time bolstered by government funding from a levy approved by voters the previous November. The center features more than three hundred exhibits designed for "children of all ages."

6

THE TOLEDO MUD HENS

BIRDS WITH NINE LIVES

Babe Ruth pitched against Ty Cobb in Toledo. Mickey Mantle hit for the cycle against the Mud Hens. Cy Young pitched in Toledo's Swayne Field. Casey Stengel led the Mud Hens to a minor-league World Series championship.

America's pastime has been played in Toledo since before the Civil War, and the Toledos, the city's first professional team, won their minor-league pennant during their inaugural season in 1883. Baseball has been a Toledo tradition ever since, despite a few seasons when there was no pro team.

Today, the Toledo Mud Hens boast one of the most recognizable names in minor-league ball. The team plays in a downtown ballpark voted the

Mud Hens outfielder Charles "Piano Legs" Hickman is featured on this 1911 tobacco card. *Courtesy of the Library of Congress.*

Fred Abbott was the Mud Hens' first baseman from 1906 to 1910. *Courtesy of the Library of Congress.*

best in all of minor-league ball. The AAA franchise has been the Detroit Tigers' top farm club since 1987. An average of 556,000 fans attend every season since the team moved into Fifth Third Field in 2002.

Some of the greatest names in baseball have played in Toledo, either for the Mud Hens or for their opponents, on their way up or on their way down from the majors. Some superstars played for Toledo briefly to rehab from injuries, and a few legends played exhibition games in the city.

The list of Mud Hens who went on to become big-league stars or major-league managers is a long one, including Casey Stengel, Bobby Murcer, Mike Marshall, Travis Fryman, Phil Hiatt, Jose Lima, Frank Viola, Horace Clark, Hack Wilson, Jim Bunning, Dazzy Vance, Kirby Puckett, Joe McCarthy, Bill Terry and Addie Joss. Jim Thorpe, the 1912 Olympic pentathlon and decathlon gold medal winner, played for the Mud Hens in 1921 and hit three home runs in a game on July 13. Byron Nelson, the golf legend, played the outfield for the Mud Hens in a 1942 exhibition game.

One of baseball's all-time greats, Mickey Mantle, played against the Mud Hens after being sent down to the Yankees' Kansas City farm team in 1951. Mantle was just nineteen years old when he told *Sporting News* that his most outstanding performance at the time was in Toledo, on July 31, 1951, when he hit two home runs, a triple and a double and came to bat in the ninth inning needing a single to hit for the cycle. Toledo sportscaster Frank Gilhooley said KC's manager, George Selkirk, surprised Mantle by giving him the swing-away sign on a 3-0 count. He knew, and the cheering fans knew, that Mantle was just one single away from hitting for the cycle, a rare achievement in baseball. According to Gilhooley, the Mick laid down a drag bunt and was "almost to the bullpen" by the time the ball hit the first baseman's glove.

Babe Ruth played three exhibition games against the Mud Hens, once as a pitcher with the Boston Red Sox in 1917 and then with the New York Yankees in 1920 and 1928. In the 1917 game at Toledo's Swayne Field, Ruth pitched against Ty Cobb, who was playing with the Mud Hens temporarily while making his way north to Detroit. Ruth hit three home runs in Toledo, including a grand slam and one that flew over the right-field fence to land on Detroit Avenue. His Yankee teammate Lou Gehrig, normally a first baseman, played the outfield in that game, according to Husman's definitive book *Baseball in Toledo*.

Cy Young, for whom the major leagues' Pitcher of the Year award is named, played in Toledo a number of times and, in 1947, at age eighty, threw a ceremonial pitch from the mound (and was paid forty dollars for the appearance).

Toledo's first professional baseball team was simply called the Toledos and made its debut in the Northwestern League, a minor league, on May 5, 1883. Dressed in blue and white uniforms, Toledo played its home games at League Park, a newly built stadium on the north side of Monroe Street, between Thirteenth and Fifteenth Streets. The Toledos got off to a fast start, winning fifty-five games and losing twenty-eight that year, beating the Saginaw Old Golds to win the Northwestern League pennant.

Success brought a promotion to the major leagues the next year, when Toledo joined the American Association. Home games were played at League Park.

Toledo's baseball record during the rest of the nineteenth century was "chaotic, to say the least," said Husman, the Mud Hens' official team historian. Over the next sixteen years, the Toledo teams had seven different names and played on nine different home fields in seven different leagues, missing a few years due to financial problems. But the Toledos, upon their promotion to the major leagues in 1884, played an important role in baseball history.

The team's catcher was Moses Fleetwood "Fleet" Walker, who had starred at Oberlin College and played ball for the University of Michigan while studying law. He came to Toledo and made his major-league debut on May 1, 1884. Walker played in forty-two games that year, hitting .263

with no home runs and leading the American Association in passed balls with seventy-two.

Statistically speaking, Walker's 1884 season for the Toledos was nothing sensational. But by playing in the American Association, Walker became the first African American in history to play on a major-league team. Although he broke the color barrier sixty-three years before Jackie Robinson donned a Dodgers uniform, Walker's place in history is often obscured because it happened before baseball's modern era.

After the season, rival team owners banded together and successfully demanded that Walker and his younger brother Welday, who had joined the Toledos during the season, be banned from Toledo's roster. Banished from the majors, Fleet continued to play minor-league ball. The New York Giants were impressed by his skills after an exhibition game in 1888 and tried to sign him to a major-league contract, but once again, the other owners and managers blocked the way.

The integration opponents were led by Chicago Cubs player-manager Cap Anson, whose bigotry was well documented. In 1883, Anson threatened to cancel an exhibition game between Chicago and Toledo unless Walker was benched. Toledo manager Charles Morton had been planning to sit Walker because the catcher had suffered a hand injury, but after Anson's racist antics, Morton defiantly put Walker in the game as an outfielder. Facing the loss of gate receipts if the game were canceled, the Cubs gave in and played. But Anson, who was born in Iowa and graduated from the University of Notre Dame, continued to do all he could to keep black players out of the majors, effectively renewing the color barrier until Jackie Robinson's historic 1947 season.

The Toledo team's 1885 season was cut short by financial woes, a common occurrence in the early years of pro baseball. There was no team in Toledo until 1888, when the Toledo Maumees competed in the Tri-State League. Both the team and the league were very weak, according to Husman—and so was attendance. Fans had a difficult time getting to the home games at Presque Isle Park, on the east side of the Maumee River near its mouth and reachable only by ferry. Team owner George Ketcham, a banker and owner of the famous trotting horse Cresceus, donated land for a new ballpark at Cherry Street and Franklin Avenue—near today's St. Vincent Medical Center—seeking to boost attendance. He named the stadium after his new yacht, Speranza Park.

The next year, baseball returned to Toledo with a new team name and a new league: the Black Pirates of the Maumee, playing in the International

League. Morton returned as manager, and after leading the team to another winning season, Toledo was promoted to the major leagues in 1890.

The Black Pirates of Toledo, competing in the American Association once again, were responsible for an interesting piece of baseball trivia: the creation of the widely used term "Texas leaguer." According to the Roger Bresnahan/ Mud Hens Chapter of the Society for American Baseball Research, Toledo player Arthur Sunday, who had played in the Texas League the year before, hit .398 for the Black Pirates. Many of his base hits were bloop singles that dropped just over the infielders' heads. An unknown Toledo sportswriter called Sunday's hits "Texas leaguers," and the term caught on.

Many of the nineteenth-century Toledo ballparks lived short lives. In addition to League Park (1883–85), Presque Isle (1888) and Speranza Park (1888–90), Toledo played at:

- Riverside Park, just south of Toledo near the Maumee River (1885).
- Olympic Park, at Indiana Avenue, Hawley Street and Woodland Avenue (1892).
- Ewing Street Park, at Ewing Street and Pinewood Avenue (1894–96).
- Whitestocking Park, on Lagrange Street at Pearl Street (1894–95).
- Bay View Park, just north of Toledo on Lake Erie (1896–1900).
- Armory Park, at Spielbusch Avenue and Orange Street next to the National Guard Armory (1897–1909).

Meanwhile, Toledo ordinances were on the books banning baseball from being played in the city on Sundays. On April 6, 1890, prodded by the Law Enforcement League, police chief Edward O'Dwyer arrested the players for both the Toledo and Wheeling teams for playing ball on Sunday. The athletes were fined two dollars each.

Toledo clergy were crusading against Sunday baseball. On April 13, Reverend J.A.P. McGaw of First Presbyterian Church preached a sermon titled "A Sabbath for Amusement Means a Sabbath for Toil," in which he said that "nothing is more certain than that God did not give the Sabbath as a day of amusement." A real estate salesman, W.H. Bishop, said at a meeting of the Law Enforcement League that "the national game was a national crime breeder."

There was no pro ball in Toledo in 1891, but the issue rose to the fore again in 1892, when ballplayers were arrested twice for playing games on Sunday—on May 22 and May 29. At the latter game, detectives wrote down "the names of prominent persons present."

The Ministers' Union, meanwhile, called baseball "a disturber of our city and a demoralizer of the young." When Mayor V.J. Emmick spoke in favor of Sunday baseball, calling it a wholesome enjoyment, the wrath of the Ministers' Union was stirred. Reverend T.S. Buckingham of the Eleventh Street Church of Christ said, "After wise and great hearted Christian men had laid the foundation of this state in the eternal laws of God, to have their degenerate offspring undo the magnificent work is but insuring [*sic*] for this country the curse of Almighty God."

Reverend S.D. Hutsinpiller of St. Paul's Methodist Church compared Mayor Emmick to Pontius Pilate and the team's owner, John Gunnels, to Judas. Gunnels asserted that without Sunday baseball, there was not enough income to keep the Toledo team in business. The Western League disbanded on July 7, and Toledo had no professional baseball club in 1893.

Sunday blue laws became an issue again in 1895, when the Toledo White Stockings played its home games at Ewing Street Park. The new park was centrally located, served by four trolley lines and within walking distance from downtown. Team president Dennis Long expected attendance to double and was convinced that the ban on Sunday baseball would not be enforced. But Ewing Park was in a busy residential neighborhood, bordered by Indiana Avenue and Dorr Street, and the noise and congestion on game day wasn't well received by all of the residents. Long didn't help matters by allowing fans onto the field after games, where they created a "rowdy atmosphere," according to the Mud Hens SABR chapter.

Neighbors filed complaints claiming that the games were disturbing their Sunday rest, and when the team arrived at Ewing Park on June 16, its first scheduled Sunday game that season, Long received a court injunction forbidding all Sunday games inside the city limits.

To avoid confrontations with police, and with hopes of boosting revenue, the Toledo team in 1885 began playing its Sunday games at Riverside Park, just south of the city line. From 1896 to 1900, it played all of its Saturday and Sunday games at the Bay View Park, also known as Casino Park, a new field north of Toledo, at Manhattan Boulevard and Summit Street.

Long grew weary of fighting Toledo's blue laws—and the impact they had on ticket sales—and lacking the funds to build a new park outside the city limits, he moved the team after the 1895 season to Terre Haute, Indiana, where it was renamed the Hottentots. The city of thirty thousand had made a strong pitch by promising attendance of two thousand every Sunday or it would make up the difference in the gate receipts.

Armory Park was the Mud Hens' home field from 1987 to 1907. The right field was so close that balls hit over it were ruled doubles. *Collection of John Husman.*

In 1896, entrepreneur Charles Strobel purchased the team, then called the Swamp Angels. But the unique combination of blue laws and Mother Nature would lead to a historic name change midway through the season. Bay View Park was built on a marsh, and its scores of American coots, a duck-like waterborne bird, flocked to the swampy grounds (now the site of a retirees' golf course). Coots were commonly called mud hens, and the Toledo team's owners took note of the nickname and officially rechristened the Toledo Swamp Angels as the Toledo Mud Hens, with the new team name making its debut on July 16, 1896.

From 1897 to 1902, weekday games were played at Armory Park on Spielbusch Avenue downtown, and Saturday and Sunday games were played at Bay View Park, which was easy for fans to reach because it was at the northern end of the Toledo Electric Street Railway Company's Summit Street line.

Over the next several years, the Mud Hens lineup included several players who made their marks in Toledo baseball history. Addie Joss, a future Hall of Famer, played for the team in 1900 and 1901 before reaching the big leagues. In two seasons, Joss—nicknamed "the Human Hairpin"—started eighty-one games, won forty-four and lost thirty-four and had an ERA of 1.61, pitching a total of 621.1 innings—numbers that are startling compared to those of the modern era. When he wasn't playing ball, Joss worked as a sportswriter for the *Toledo News-Bee* newspaper.

Another memorable player of the era was Elmer Stricklett, credited with being the inventor of the spitball, who pitched for the Mud Hens in 1900. The new pitch apparently worked like a charm, as Stricklett gave up just six hits and two runs in 126 innings, according to baseball-reference.com.

Professional baseball began to settle down in Toledo—and elsewhere—after the turn of the century, with less turmoil and fewer financial disasters. Toledo joined with seven other teams in 1902 to form the minor-league American Association, whose teams stayed essentially the same for the next five decades.

Samuel "Golden Rule" Jones, who was elected mayor in 1897, stopped enforcing the Sunday ban on baseball and other public events in 1902, explaining that he was elected to do the bidding of the citizens, and if they wanted Sunday amusements he would allow it.

From 1902 to 1909, the Mud Hens played all their home games at Armory Park, a stadium with plenty of quirks. One large section of the left field wall was the castle-like National Guard Armory, a towering brick edifice topped with battlements. It had a curved corner tower that was in the field of play, and the park's right wall was so close to the hitters that any ball hit over the wall was scored a double, not a home run.

In 1911, Armory Park played host to a revival led by former major-league baseball player Billy Sunday, who gave up his baseball career in the 1880s to become a Christian minister. A temporary wood-frame tabernacle with seating for 11,000 was erected on the ballpark grounds at a cost of $10,000. Three revival meetings were held daily, except on Mondays, from April 8 through May 21, with 7,323 conversions reported during the six-week revival. While in Toledo, Sunday preached the funeral for former Mud Hen and Cleveland major-league pitching star Addie Joss. More than 5,000 people, including Ty Cobb, Cy Young and the entire Cleveland and Detroit major-league teams, turned out to pay their respects.

Armory Park burned down in 1934, reportedly in connection with the violence over that year's historic Auto-Lite strike. Today, the federal courthouse sits on the Spielbusch Avenue site.

The Mud Hens were purchased in 1908 by William Armour, who played for the Black Pirates in 1892. He had managed teams in Cleveland and Detroit, where he signed Ty Cobb to a $700 bonus and $200 monthly salary, before returning to Toledo to manage the Mud Hens and run the team's business. His financial partner was Charles Somers, a millionaire businessman from Cleveland, who played a key role in establishing the American League as a major-league rival to the National League. Somers, whose family made a fortune in the coal business, was vice-president of the American League from 1901 to 1906 and bankrolled a number of new franchises, including ones in Philadelphia, Chicago and Boston.

In 1908, Armour began scouting for a Toledo site on which to build a stadium larger than Armory Park, which had a seating capacity of approximately 4,500. Fans were turned away every Saturday because there were no seats available.

Noah H. Swayne Jr., a Toledo lawyer and businessman, had purchased property at Monroe Street and Detroit Avenue for $47,000, and in March 1909 leased it to the Mud Hens' parent company, Toledo Exhibition Company, for $1,902 a year plus Swayne's exclusive use of a private box with six seats.

That led to the construction of Swayne Field, a state-of-the-art ballpark that would be the home of Toledo baseball for the next forty-six years. Construction began on March 6, 1909, and crews worked around the clock, under the bright light of arc lamps, finishing the job in less than four months and easily meeting the deadline for the July 3 opener against Columbus. While most stadiums of the era were built of wood, the grandstands in the new Toledo park were made of steel and reinforced concrete and were touted as being fireproof.

Armour, backed by Somers, invested an estimated $125,000 in the building, which had a seating capacity of 11,900. The park had a twelve-foot exterior wall made of concrete, which, according to Husman, "was there to keep people out, not to hit the ball over." (Although the park was demolished in 1956, a section of the left field fence still stands, between a strip mall and a car wash.)

Opening day at Swayne Field, July 3, 1909, featured an eighteen-inning thriller with Columbus defeating the Mud Hens 12–11. *Collection of John Husman.*

It would take a prodigious hit to clear the outfield fences in most of the park, with the left-field wall being 380 feet away and the center field wall measuring 505 feet from home plate. Only the right-field fence, at 326 feet, was within reasonable reach. But in the "dead ball era" of the early 1900s, most home runs were inside-the-park hits, with only a few clearing the fences. "There were a lot of long hits, a lot of outfield play and a lot of running in the game in those days," Husman said. An article about the new park in the *Blade* commented that "with this big place to play there ought to be some swell clouting."

Tickets for opening day ranged from seventy-five cents for grandstand seats to twenty-five cents for the bleachers, and the game drew a crowd of 9,350. Although it wasn't a sellout, at the time, it was the largest crowd ever to watch a baseball game in Toledo. The Mud Hens and Columbus played an eighteen-inning thriller, lasting more than three and a half hours before the visiting team came out on top with a 12–11 victory.

Husman, who is a lifelong Mud Hen fan as well as the team historian, said he attended "countless" games as a youngster with his grandfather, who lived on Virginia Street in the Old West End, just a short walk from the stadium. "They really did a great job building that park," he said. "The first concrete-and-steel stadium in the majors was Shibe Park in Philadelphia, which opened the same year. So it was right up there with the best."

Adding to the park's personality was a Toledo Edison smokestack bearing the words "Heat, Light and Power" and a huge pile of coal beyond the left-field fence. The scoreboard had slots for the numbers to be manually inserted like the one still in use at Boston's Fenway Park. The gates at Swayne Field were opened late in the game allowing free admission to all. Anyone who caught a ball outside the park and returned it was given a free pass to a game. After the game ended, fans could walk across the playing field to exit through a gate in the right-field fence.

Although baseball in Toledo was relatively stable after the opening of Swayne Field, there were some ups and downs. Somers moved the Toledo Mud Hens to Cleveland in 1914 and renamed them the Spiders. It was believed to have been a preemptive move by Somers to keep the upstart Federal League from establishing a Cleveland franchise. Somers had the schedule arranged so that one of his two Cleveland teams was always playing at home, and it succeeded in keeping the Federal League from fielding a team in the city.

But the fallout for Toledo was that it had no Mud Hens team in 1914 or 1915. A Class C minor-league team called the Toledo Soumichers (for

Southern Michigan) played at Swayne Field in the first half of 1914, but attendance was so poor that the team played all its games on the road for the second half of the season. After winning just nine games and losing fifty-eight, the Soumichers disbanded.

Roger Bresnahan, a Toledo native, former Mud Hen and major-league catcher (and the only Toledoan enshrined in baseball's Hall of Fame), brought baseball back to Toledo in 1916. The *Blade* ran a contest to name the team, and the Mud Hens won over such suggestions as the Rajahs or the Bresna Hens. But the team owners felt that with the new start the team should have a new name and called the team the Iron Men. That name lasted until 1918, when the Mud Hens name was reinstated.

Hall of Famer Charles Dillon "Casey" Stengel was a player-manager for the Toledo Mud Hens, leading them to the Junior World Series title in 1927. *Toledo–Lucas County Public Library.*

One of the finest eras in Mud Hens history began in 1926, when Charles Dillon "Casey" Stengel, a colorful personality and a fan favorite, was named the team's player-manager. Stengel hit .328 in eighty-eight games his first year with the Mud Hens, and the next year, he led a veteran squad to the American Association championship. According to the Mud Hens SABR chapter, Stengel played just eighteen games in 1927, but one of those was particularly noteworthy: he put himself in as pinch-hitter in the eleventh inning with the bases loaded and Toledo trailing 9–8, and Stengel connected for a grand slam. It was his only home run for Toledo and the last of his professional career. Stengel led the Toledo club to the Junior World Series title in 1927. He managed the Mud Hens through 1931.

Several Negro League teams also played their home games at Swayne Field, including the Tigers in 1923, the Crawfords in 1939 and the Cubs in 1945. They'd use the stadium when the Mud Hens were on the road.

In 1928, bleachers were added in center field, increasing seating capacity to fifteen thousand. Lights were added in 1933, and the first night game at Swayne Field was played on June 23, 1933, two years before the Cincinnati Reds became the first major-league team to play under the lights. Another significant change came in 1945, when an inner fence was installed, giving hitters a better chance to clear the wall for a home run.

As the major leagues began to develop the farm system in the minor leagues, training players for the big leagues, the Mud Hens became affiliated with a series of parent teams, including the Cleveland Indians, Detroit Tigers, St. Louis Browns and the Milwaukee Braves. When the Braves moved their top minor-league team to Toledo in 1953, team owners decided to hold a contest for a new name. Fred W. Schultz, a Toledo bus driver, submitted the winning entry, the Glass Sox, a reference to Toledo's famous glass industry and its "Glass City" nickname. Schultz won two season passes "and the wrath of almost everyone in the Toledo area," Husman wrote.

Fans protested, and Toledo City Council even petitioned the team for reconsideration. As a compromise, the name "Glass" was dropped and the team became "the Toledo Sox."

During the Sox era, with the Milwaukee Braves affiliation, the Mud Hens won the 1953 American Association pennant, losing to the Kansas City Blues in the playoffs. Attendance skyrocketed from 41,497 in 1952 to 343,614 in '53.

But the Toledo teams' last games at Swayne Field were played on September 5, 1955, when the Sox hosted the Indianapolis Indians in a double-header. Toledo lost the first game 3–2 and then won the nightcap 2–1 in twelve innings. Attendance was a scant 1,748. Nobody knew it would be the final curtain for Swayne Field.

The Braves moved the team to Wichita after the '55 season, a decision that left Toledo baseball fans stunned and angry. Attendance had been solid, and the Toledo Sox were playing well; fans were given no indication that a move was pending. Toledo real estate agent Allie Reuben, who bought Swayne Field in 1933, sold it to the Kroger Company, which demolished Swayne Field in 1956 to build a grocery store.

After a nine-year absence, the Mud Hens returned to the Toledo area in 1965 and played at the Lucas County Recreation Center. *Collection of John Husman.*

There was no professional ball in Toledo for the next nine years. The closest pro teams were all in the major leagues and at least an hour's drive away. The long drought ended as suddenly as it began, with the announcement in the spring of 1965 that the New York Yankees' top minor-league team would be moving from Richmond, Virginia, to the Toledo area and would play in Maumee, a suburb south of the city. The team would once again be called the Mud Hens.

It was a hurried deal, and organizers hastily converted the Fort Miami Fairgrounds racetrack on Key Street into a suitable baseball park. The racetrack's existing grandstands were modified for use along the third base side on Key Street, new stands were built behind home plate and first base and the playing field was groomed into shape by the time the 1965 season started.

The locker rooms and facilities at the Lucas County Recreation Center were well below standard, however. The ballplayers had to walk from the locker rooms through an aisle lined with fans to get to the field. It was a wonderful arrangement for the fans who wanted autographs or to talk to the players but a headache for players trying to get ready for a game.

The return of the Toledo Mud Hens was largely credited to Ned Skeldon, who was vice-mayor of Toledo when the team moved away and later was elected a Lucas County commissioner. His efforts to save Swayne Field failed. He put a bond issue on the ballot for a new stadium, but it was rejected by voters. Skeldon continued to lead the efforts to bring baseball back to Toledo, and in appreciation of his tireless efforts, the Maumee baseball park was dedicated as the Ned Skeldon Stadium on June 28, 1988.

The Mud Hens' affiliation with the New York Yankees lasted just two seasons, followed by arrangements with the Tigers (1967–73), Phillies (1974–75) and Twins (1979–86) before the Tigers returned and made Toledo their AAA farm team again in 1987, an arrangement that has continued ever since. Attendance in the Tigers' second reign improved dramatically, from an average of 169,000 in the ten previous seasons to 258,000 over the next ten years as the Tigers affiliate.

Much of the credit for the new success went to Gene Cook, the team's general manager. He helped make the Mud Hens a household name in the United States and beyond by enlisting Toledo-born actor Jamie Farr to wear Mud Hens gear on the hit show *M*A*S*H*, which was a ratings sensation from 1972 to 1983. Cook also had the vision to bring the Mud Hens back to Toledo, leaving the ill-appointed Skeldon Stadium behind for a new ballpark in the city's Warehouse District, bordered by Washington, Huron, Monroe and St. Clair Streets.

On April 9, 2002, the Toledo Mud Hens played its first game against the Norfolk Tide in Fifth Third Field, the naming rights purchased by Fifth Third Bank. The $39 million stadium features computer-aligned seating with all 8,943 seats angled toward the middle of the field, a spacious concourse lined with a wide variety of food and drink vendors, views of the cityscape beyond the outfield walls and an asymmetrical design, creating a distinctive blend of old and new baseball architecture. *Newsweek* magazine named it the "Best Ballpark in Minor League Baseball" in 2002.

In the first thirteen years in the new stadium, attendance averaged more than 550,000 a year. The team sells twenty-five thousand T-shirts, twenty thousand hats and forty-nine thousand Mud Hens novelties a year. The success of the Mud Hens in downtown Toledo has given new life to a once dreary downtown, with new restaurants, bars and entertainment venues opening up in the area. In March 2015, the Toledo Plan Commission unanimously approved plans for a $19 million festival and events park called

"Hensville," to be developed near the stadium. The new entertainment district will have a patio area, a fountain, a lawn and landscaped areas and a building for special events. There will be three rooftop patios, including two with views of Fifth-Third Field. Scheduled to be ready for opening day in 2016, Hensville is expected to draw 150,000 people a year.

Joe Napoli, the Mud Hens' general manager since 1999, said the idea is "to create another vibrant and active, exciting place to go."

7
SOUNDS OF THE CITY

ALL THAT JAZZ (AND ROCK)

In September 1994, Russian musician Georgy Palmov walked through the doors of Rusty's Jazz Café with his mandolin case in hand, came to an abrupt halt and stared, wide-eyed and smiling, as he turned in a slow circle to gaze at his surroundings. "I can't believe I'm standing here…in *Rusty's!*" he said reverently. The Moscow musician, who was touring the United States with the Russian bluegrass band Kukuruza, had been counting the days until he took the stage at Rusty's. Long before the Internet shrunk the world's borders, Rusty's had caught Palmov's attention in Russia, and the mandolin player had been dreaming of the day he would play at Toledo's funkiest jazz joint.

"Anywhere you go, if you tell them you're from Toledo and if they're involved with jazz at all, they always ask about Rusty's," said Chris Buzzelli, a jazz professor at Bowling Green State University who played frequently at Rusty's. "People all over the country know about that club."

And Rusty's was not the only Toledo-area music club with a following that went far beyond the city limits. Contrary to the lyrics of John Denver's 1975 hit song "Saturday Night in Toledo, Ohio," which jokes that the city's entertainment highlight is to "go to the bakery and watch the buns rise," generations of Toledoans have enjoyed and supported a vibrant music scene.

Many successful musicians got their starts playing at Toledo nightclubs, and scores of famous artists have entertained crowds in the city's many colorful, cozy and convenient clubs. Art Tatum, widely considered the greatest jazz pianist who ever lived, was born in Toledo in 1909 and has influenced

The first Rusty's Jazz Café opened on Secor Road in 1963, featuring live jazz seven nights a week. *Toledo–Lucas County Public Library.*

generations of musicians. Before moving to New York and achieving global fame, Tatum spotted the talent in a neighborhood kid named Jon Hendricks and mentored the youngster, who went on to win five Grammy Awards as a jazz singer and lyricist.

Some of the most well-known and cherished venues have faded into history but are still fondly remembered by musicians and music fans alike. Along with Rusty's, some of the clubs that still trigger warm memories among Toledo music fans include the Kin Wa Low, the Trianon Ballroom, the Aku-Aku Polynesian Room, Murphy's Place, the Asylum (later renamed Club Bijou), the Ottawa Tavern and the Peppermint Club. The area's most famous blues venue, Hines Farm, was closed for years but has been struggling back to new life.

Rusty's Jazz Café was a genuine, if improbable, jazz gem. Tucked into a side street lined with car repair shops and warehouses, the only tip-off to passing motorists that Tedrow Road had something special was an honorary street sign designating it "Jazz Avenue." Despite the industrial backdrop, the South Toledo jazz club was an artistic hot spot where live music could be heard seven nights a week.

From world-renowned jazz artists Wynton Marsalis, Maynard Ferguson, David Sanborn, Red Rodney and Gerry Mulligan to the finest local musicians, including Gene Parker, Jimmy Cook, John Mast, Jean Holden, Scott Potter, Jim Gottron and Ramona Collins, Rusty's was a magnet for top-notch musical talent for four decades.

The club's enduring popularity was directly attributable to the dedication of its owner, Margaret "Rusty" Monroe, an irrepressible advocate of jazz and the people who create that unique, American-born art form. "Rusty's was an institution, and *Rusty* was an institution," said Jon Richardson, former president of the Toledo Jazz Society. "If it were not for Rusty Monroe, Toledo would not have had the opportunity to hear all this wonderful jazz for so many years—for generations, really."

Monroe, nicknamed for her fiery red hair, had a difficult childhood growing up in rural Ohio. Her mother died when she was ten, and her father died when she was fourteen. Rusty graduated early from high school, at age fourteen, and the next year married a man who had a serious gambling problem. "If two birds landed on a telephone wire, he'd bet which one would fly off first," Monroe once said.

After a divorce, she moved to Hollywood, California, where she worked as a waitress and barmaid while pursuing an acting career. As a single mother with three children, she eventually decided she couldn't devote the time needed to be an actress and moved her family back to Ohio. Monroe was in her forties when she discovered jazz, attending a Toledo concert by Dinah Washington. "After that, I was hooked," she said.

With the knowledge she had gleaned in California, Monroe felt confident that she could run her own club and restaurant, and in 1963, at age forty-four, she opened the first Rusty's Jazz Café on Secor Road, near the Westgate Village Shopping Center. In 1979, after a short break between clubs, she opened her second jazz venue in a small, stand-alone building on Tedrow Road in South Toledo.

"I wasn't afraid of hard work, and I wanted to give the musicians a place to play," Monroe said. She started with just a piano in a corner and an open invitation to local jazz artists. The club's reputation grew quickly, and once the jazz community got involved, the music never stopped. Rusty's featured live music seven nights a week, three hundred and sixty four days a year—it was closed only on Christmas Day.

"It wasn't about making a million dollars," Monroe said. "I knew jazz was never a big draw, but it's an art form. It comes from the heart. And it will never go away."

Monroe said she knew her way around the kitchen, and she knew that jazz artists didn't have a lot of money. So she began cooking home-style meals at the club and selling them at ridiculously low prices. "With musicians, you have to remember the word 'affordable.' We started out with fifty-cent spaghetti nights. Then we had to go to a dollar and a half," she said.

She also kept the cover charge as low as possible, and for years, the seats at the rear of her club were free. That rear section was often filled by high school students, many of whom received extra credit for going to a jazz show at the venue. Reluctantly, Monroe ended the free-seat tradition in 2000, only because "it became necessary to pay the band a little better."

How many hours a week did Monroe work at her jazz club? "Let's put it this way," she said. "If I wasn't at the club, I took it home with me and slept with it. It was the last thing I did at night and the first thing in the morning."

Men's Journal magazine in the early 2000s named Rusty's Jazz Café one of the "50 Best Bars in America."

The club on Tedrow Road was long and narrow, with a small stage decorated with loops of silver garland hanging from the ceiling. The room had an eclectic and homey feel to it, decorated with jazz photos and posters. A buffet table was set up near the entrance, and the raised level at the back of the room featured tables with chessboards and chess pieces. Along the side of the room, a fireplace blazed away, and patrons were invited to toast marshmallows.

When Wynton Marsalis came by after a concert in Toledo, he and Monroe sat around a table and talked for hours. "He saw the young people and said it was a wonderful thing I was doing," Monroe recalled. "He saw that I was reaching ahead, helping build the future of jazz."

Eddie Abrams, Rusty's pianist for twenty-three years, was known for his encouragement of—and patience with—young musicians. "He was the man in charge," Toledo trumpeter Jimmy Cook once said. "No matter what you played or how you played, he'd give you a chance to play. He put up with some really bad stuff at times!"

Tim Ries, a jazz saxophonist who has been playing in the Rolling Stones' touring band for fifteen years, is from nearby Tecumseh, Michigan. He polished his jazz skills at Rusty's, starting before he was old enough to get a driver's license. When he was fourteen, his parents would drive him to Toledo two or three nights a week to play at the club. "It was a huge learning experience for me," Ries said.

Rusty's Jazz Café supported young musicians—even if they weren't playing jazz. Monroe allowed local rock bands, including the Sprags and the Stain, to play on Sunday nights, saying with a wink that "I guess you could call it jazz-rock."

Maynard Ferguson, one of the most famous jazz trumpeters, helped spread the word about Rusty's Café to jazz artists and aficionados everywhere. "He really put us on the map," Cook recalled. "He told everybody, from Sweden to San Francisco, that he was never treated so well in his whole life."

Whenever Ferguson—or any other touring band—played at her club, Monroe would hand each band member a carryout box on their way out containing a home-cooked meal.

Alexander Zonjic, the jazz flutist from Windsor, Ontario, would bring his full band to Toledo to play at Rusty's, rather than play as a solo artist, even though he often lost money on the gig. He didn't mind because he thought so highly of the club and its owner. Zonjic laughed about having to stack up the speakers and squeeze all the instruments and musicians together to fit onto the stage.

Jon Hendricks, a Toledo native who has won five Grammy Awards, played at Rusty's whenever he was back in his hometown. "Rusty, to me, she's like one of the heroes of Stalingrad," he said. "She's kept the heathen at bay for as long as she was in that club, and she dispensed American culture every night. Who else can say that? I love Rusty—as do a lot of people."

Rusty managed to keep the heathen at bay until 2003, when she sold the club and retired in Florida. She was eighty-four years old and "wanted to leave it at the top." The new owner had planned to continue the club's jazz tradition, but after a few months transformed the building into a sports bar.

Gene Parker, one of the giants of the Toledo jazz scene, lamented the closing of Rusty's. "Size doesn't make any difference when it comes to art," Parker said. "That was a little place, it looked like a hole in the wall, but the effects were felt all over the world."

Toledo musicians held a "Rusty's Jazz Picnic" in Toledo every summer after the club closed, and Monroe attended every year until 2008, when she said she was too ill to make the trip from Florida. "I've had a great run," she said, "but now that I'm older I've settled down a little." A few months later, in October 2008, she died at age eighty-nine.

In the early 1990s, a leading jazz magazine reported that, aside from New York City, there were forty clubs in the United States that focused solely on jazz. And Toledo had two of them: Rusty's Jazz Café and Murphy's Place.

"It was an embarrassment of riches" for Toledo jazz fans, said Jon Richardson, attorney and former president of the Toledo Jazz Society.

While Rusty's was presenting live jazz in a suburban setting, Murphy's Place opened in 1991 on Madison Avenue, in the heart of downtown Toledo's financial district. The club was based in a narrow, Tudor-style building with a low stage set in the middle of the room. The owners, bassist Clifford Murphy and his longtime partner, Joan Russell, designed the club to incorporate some of their favorite elements of the many venues they had visited over the years. They met in the early 1970s when Clifford was traveling with the Murphys Trio, and the group toured constantly, with Russell managing the business part of the music. "When we were traveling, all we did was wake up the next day and rehearse and play that night and go to the next site, next state. Same ol', same ol'," Murphy recalled.

Murphy's Place opened in 1991 on Madison Avenue before relocating to Fort Industry Square on Water Street in 1996. *Author's collection.*

They chose to settle down in Toledo, Murphy's hometown, and opened their club with the Murphys as the house band. Clifford, a quiet and confident bandleader, played bass, and his longtime musical colleague, Detroit-born Claude Black, was featured on piano. A lightning-quick, creative pianist, Black had performed with such jazz luminaries as Charlie "Bird" Parker, Stan Getz, Joe Henderson and Wes Montgomery and was Aretha Franklin's musical director from 1965 to 1967.

Murphy's Place relocated in 1996 to a waterfront venue in Fort Industry Square, just a few blocks east of the Madison Avenue club. The site, at 151 Water Street, previously was known as Digby's Pub. The basement-level club was a cozy room with dark-wood accents and large impressionistic portraits

Bassist Clifford Murphy was co-owner of Murphy's Place, which closed after his partner, Joan Russell, passed away in 2011. *Courtesy of Leslie Cusano.*

of famous jazz artists painted on frosted glass that was lit up from behind, giving the club a warm glow. Intimate seating for the fans was available on three sides of the stage. Rows of tables on a second tier looked down over a bannister to the stage below.

Together, Clifford and Claude created musical magic six nights a week at Murphy's Place. The pair had been playing together since the early 1950s, and by the time Murphy's Place opened, the duo estimated that they knew more than three thousand songs, with a performance-ready repertoire of about seven hundred tunes. But every song was a unique adventure, a one-of-a-kind artistic moment. Asked if they ever played the same song the same way twice, Black bristled. "No, no, no, no, no, no, no, no, no, NO!" he said with emotion. "We play some of the same songs, but we always play them different."

The two were often joined by Glenda Biddlestone on vocals and Sean Dobbins on drums, although they had a number of singers and drummers over the years. Murphy's Place also often brought in touring artists, with Clifford and Claude providing the musical backing for many of them, including their good friends saxophonists David "Fathead" Newman and Joe Henderson. Among the other nationally known jazz artists who performed at Murphy's Place were Benny Green, Kenny Burrell, Ray Brown, Jeff Hamilton, David Liebman, Michael Wolff, Johnny O'Neal, Rachel Z and French twins Louis and Francois Moutin (who had just performed at Lincoln Center in Manhattan).

Black said playing with Murphy was like playing with a brother—they were so comfortable with each other's style. "If you're playing with your brother, you don't have to say anything. You just play," Black said. Even after fifty years of collaborating, their energy and creativity inspired and elevated each other's artistry—and kept jazz fans coming back for more.

When Russell passed away after a stroke in January 2011 at age seventy-seven, Clifford Murphy found himself in a quandary. He had always focused on the music and let Joan handle the finances. He sought to keep the club going, but it closed five months later, with a farewell bash on May 31, 2011.

"It's a real sad day for Toledo," said "Ragtime Rick" Grafing. "There's no full-time home anymore for people who are jazz fans and devoted to seeing it stay alive."

The club was jam-packed for the farewell, and some regulars griped that if just a fraction of the people who showed up for the funeral had come even occasionally, Murphy's Place would have stayed in business.

The waterfront jazz venue went through several owners after Murphy's Place closed, but as of March 2015, none had been successful, and the former jazz club was vacant.

Hines Farm

On the outskirts of Toledo, in a rural area about fifteen miles west of the city, a forty-acre plot of land became an entertainment mecca and a cultural center for African Americans in northwest Ohio.

It all started in 1937, when Frank "Sonny" Hines and his wife, Sarah, bought a two-bedroom house with a furnished basement in Swanton, Ohio, on State Route 295, which at the time was an important link between Chicago and Detroit. Frank, who was born in Kentucky in 1903, and Sarah, born in Tennessee in 1911, moved to Toledo, where they were married in 1938. The entrepreneurs began holding house parties in their basement, which had a full bar from which they sold bottles of whiskey and a turntable and speakers for blasting the latest blues recordings.

"It was everybody talking at the same time, you know, passing the bottle around," recalled Toledo blues musician Blind Bobby Smith. "Sometimes it stayed open 'til 3:00 or 3:30 a.m., Hines wishing everybody'd get out of there so he could go to bed."

The house parties continued through the late 1940s, and by 1950, the Hineses needed more room—and more sleep. Frank built a forty- by

Bluesman Blind Bobby Smith poses in front of Hines Farm, known for its music, motorcycle races, good food and good times. *Courtesy of John Gibbs Rockwood.*

thirty-foot wooden juke joint, or music club, in a heavily wooded area at the rear of the property. It had a three-foot-tall concrete platform for the musicians and a kitchen and barbecue pit that could handle two whole hogs. Barbecued ribs, chicken and catfish soon became the house specialties.

In a neighborhood known as "Moonshine Valley" for its many illegal stills, the Hineses were the first blacks in northwest Ohio to obtain a liquor license and sell beer and whiskey legally to their clientele—much to the consternation of their moonshining neighbors.

The juke joint had electricity, so musicians were able to plug in their electric instruments and amplifiers that gave the blues of the era its signature sound, loud and gritty.

The club's rural setting was a key factor in its success, according to Matthew Donahue, an author, musician and Bowling Green State University professor of popular culture. "The 1920s and 1930s saw the largest migration of African Americans in the history of the United States," Donahue said. "Often referred to as the Great Black Migration, it consisted of blacks moving from the rural South to the urban North in search of jobs and better living conditions."

Many new Toledoans landed jobs in factories, building automobiles or making parts for the auto industry. While the southerners worked in the city, they missed the country life they had left behind and were drawn to the open land and friendly people at Hines Farm.

"They had just migrated here from the South and they were just more country oriented," said Henry Griffin, who grew up in the neighborhood and bought Hines Farm in 1978. "A lot of folks felt jammed up in the city, and a lot of folks came out here to hear good music."

The Hineses charged $1.00 or $1.50, which included parking and the cover charge for the juke joint. Frank was the "keeper of the peace," checking customers for guns and knives and generally enforcing the rules ("He broke a lot of heads back then," one patron recalled), while Sarah ran the club, overseeing the kitchen and bar and booking the bands. She hung posters on telephone poles and drove around town with a car equipped with a microphone and speaker, announcing upcoming events.

During the winters, the Hineses continued holding house parties in their basement, but in 1957, Frank and his brother George began building a new club that would become a favorite in the blues world. Constructed of cement block, the new club measured 46 feet wide and 101 feet deep, and it could accommodate about five hundred people in the main room. It took a year to build and featured a horseshoe-shaped bar with glass-block supports, a number of booths and tables, a dance floor, a pool table, a juke box and a bandstand. A soul food kitchen was built next to the bar.

"They served the best catfish, the best fish dinner, the best chicken or steak dinner—whatever you wanted, you got it," said Toledo bluesman Roman Griswold.

The building had living quarters upstairs where traveling musicians could stay for free. One of their regulars was John Lee Hooker, a 1991 inductee into the Rock and Roll Hall of Fame. Hooker, who moved from Clarksdale, Mississippi, to Detroit in the 1940s, stayed at Hines Farm during the summers. "It wasn't a lot of money, but it was a lot of fun," he said. "Lot of good people and…you had a good time. It was kind of like a party thing. I wouldn't call it a show. I'd just say we were just having a party."

Toledo jazz bassist Clifford Murphy said there was just something special about Hines Farm. "When you walked into the place, you could just feel the happiness," he recalled.

Hooker, in an interview shortly before his death in 2001, described Hines Farm as "a one and only place—wasn't no other place like that I have been to that was like Hines Farm."

Among the other blues artists who played Hines Farm were B.B. King, Muddy Waters, Otis Redding, Bobby "Blue" Bland, Freddie King and Little Esther Phillips. Local blues musicians who got a chance to play at the club and hone their skills included Big Jack Reynolds, the Griswolds, the Jayhawks and Blind Bobby Smith. "One thing about playing at Hines Farm: you had to be a pretty damn good musician 'cause he wanted the best," said Toledo guitarist Art Griswold.

Blues icon B.B. King remembered Hines Farm for its "good food, good music and pretty girls. It was the only place that was happening." He played there three or four times a year during the 1950s and '60s, when Hines Farm was part of the "chitlin' circuit," a string of venues where touring African American musicians and comedians performed.

Eddie Kirkland, a Detroit blues artist, played frequently at Hines Farm. "It was a great scene, man…Oh man, it was a nice place. People came from Lima [Ohio], people came from Dayton, Columbus and Cleveland. The place was well known. It had quite a name and was happening back in the day."

The bands usually started at 10:00 p.m. on weekend nights and played until 2:30 a.m. The warm-up acts sometimes featured exotic "shake dancers" and female impersonators.

In addition to the music, Hines Farm was known for hosting big events, including horse races and exhibition baseball games by Negro League

Hines Farm featured such stars as B.B. King and Count Basie. It closed in 1976 but is being restored and holds several shows a year. *Author's collection.*

teams—including the Hines Farm All Stars, Toledo city champions the Unitcast Team and the Detroit Crystal All Stars.

Some of the most popular events at the farm were motorcycle races, drawing competitors from across the country. "Hines would send out a flier that he was having a motorcycle race," said Griffin, "and he would have people come from Georgia, Alabama, Mississippi. They'd get on their motorcycles and ride up there and there'd be thousands of 'em." Each race winner would be presented with a trophy, and many of the racers hung around after the races ended at 8:00 p.m. to attend the evening concerts. The races inspired the founding of local black motorcycle clubs, including the Gypsy Angels and the Atomic Pirates.

In addition to enjoying the entertainment as spectators, Hines Farm patrons were given a chance to participate in activities such as miniature golf, archery, hayrides, carnival rides and ice skating, and children competed in foot races and "clothesline races," where they ran after a motorcycle dragging a clothesline with the goal of snagging a piece of clothing off the rope. It was a family-friendly atmosphere during the day and a smoky blues joint at night.

In 1961, Frank Hines added a spacious outdoor patio next to the main club that became known as "Mr. Luke's Outdoor Pavilion." The concrete patio featured an elevated, covered bandstand at one end for the performers and picnic tables and an open dance area for the patrons. The patio held a grand opening celebration on August 13, 1961, with the Count Basie Orchestra performing. Tickets were priced at $1.50.

The club slowly began losing its popularity after rock-and-roll started taking over the music world in the 1960s. B.B. King said that smaller clubs like Hines Farm could no longer afford to pay the top blues acts, and even if they could, "nobody would want to come because they'd rather go to a rock club."

Hines Farm closed in 1976. Sarah Hines died two years later, in 1978, and Frank Hines passed away in 1981.

Griffin, who fell in love with Hines Farm going to shows there as a child, bought the property in 1978 and devoted the next few decades to restoring the venue, one small step at a time. He reopened it for occasional concerts during the 2000s and held an annual blues festival on the grounds. After his death in January 2013, the property went through a probate court for ten months before it was awarded to Griffin's son, Steve Coleman. He said he plans to restore Hines Farm to pristine condition and wants to "keep the tradition alive."

KIN WA LOW AND AKU-AKU

Would you like a plate of chop suey with your Ella Fitzgerald tune? How about a lobster dinner and a Phyllis Diller joke?

For decades, some of Toledo's favorite entertainment venues were supper clubs where patrons could order a good meal and enjoy entertainment by some of the biggest names in show business. Places such as the Bon-Ton, Ka-Sees and the Crescent Club spring to mind for many Toledoans, but two of the supper clubs with exotic names have earned legendary status in local lore: the Kin Wa Low and the Aku-Aku Polynesian Room.

The Kin Wa Low, a Chinese name that translates as "lovely flowering palace," was founded in 1913 by Ha Sun Loo in a storefront at Cherry and Huron Streets and then expanded to include three dining rooms that could seat up to two hundred guests at a time. It grew into Toledo's "very best" supper club, according to historian Clint Mauk, who called it "top-notch and romantic…It made couples feel they were in a special world or in the movies. Prom nights were always a big feature."

High school students who saved up for a big night at the Kin Wa Low would often spend just a few dollars on their meals and then sip five-cent Cokes the rest of the night to watch the entertainment. They were treated like millionaires, though, as the supper club's owners believed that it was important to make a good impression on their "customers of the future."

In addition to the tables and booths for dinner, the Kin Wa Low had a dance floor and a small bandstand. Show times were 7:30 and 10:30 p.m. and 1:00 a.m. There was no cover charge most weeknights, although on Saturdays when local bands were performing, the club often charged fifty cents for admission—met by gripes from some customers, the owners recalled.

When a national artist played at the club, the cover was $1.50. Among the big names who performed at the Kin Wa Low, in addition to Ella Fitzgerald, were Patti Page, Bobby Darin, Helen O'Connell, the McGuire Sisters and Steve Lawrence.

Lawrence said the Toledo supper club was one of his first jobs before he became a major star as a duo with his wife, Eydie Gorme. He remembered playing the Kin Wa Low as a teenage solo artist, earning $150 a week in the mid-1950s. "That was one of my first jobs," he said. "You went down a flight of stairs, into the basement, then you'd go to the back of the restaurant where they had a little stage and a dressing area. I remember hanging out next to the Peking ducks and the guys chopping vegetables."

Lawrence loved the place, especially the Chinese food, which he ate all week long. He'd put the meals on his tab, and "at the end of the week, I'd just endorse my check and hand it over to the management," Lawrence said with a laugh.

The Kin Wa Low closed in 1962, after nearly fifty years in business. In 1968, an eight-story apartment building for senior citizens was built on the location.

The Aku-Aku Polynesian Room, a lounge and restaurant, was an integral part of the Town House Motel, built in 1960 at a cost of $750,000. Located at Bancroft Street and Detroit Avenue, on the former site of Notre Dame Academy, the motel was originally going to be called the Stardust, a reflection of its Las Vegas aspirations. The motel was an innovative design for its time, with two U-shaped stories and an Olympic-sized pool in the center court. Motel brochures boasted that the building was in "the geographical center of Toledo."

The ribbon-cutting ceremony opening the motel pool included the Aku-Aku owner Irving "Slick" Shapiro and such notables as Toledo mayor Michael Damas, Lucas County sheriff William Hirsch, attorney Sid Green, Toledo fire chief Arnold Papenhagen and *Blade* columnist Mitch Woodbury.

Dedicating the Aku-Aku/Town House pool in 1960 are, *from left*, Lucas County sheriff William Hirsch, club owner Irving "Slick" Shapiro, attorney Sidney Green, Toledo mayor Michael Damas, Sam Foreman, Toledo fire chief Arnold Papenhagen and *Blade* writer Mitch Woodbury.

Vegas comedian Jack E. Leonard performed at the Aku-Aku's black-tie grand opening on December 13, 1960, and returned for a New Year's Eve engagement where tickets sold for $100.

Over the next ten years, the Aku-Aku featured many of the biggest names in the entertainment world. The stars who performed at the club—many for lengthy or repeated engagements—included comedians Phyllis Diller, Dick Gregory, Bill Dana and Henny Youngman and such musical legends as Count Basie, Duke Ellington, Buddy Rich, Woody Herman, Carmen McRae, Stan Kenton, Erskine Hawkins, Earl Bostic, Billy Eckstine, the Glenn Miller Orchestra, Harry James and Frank Sinatra Jr. The supper club also featured the top local entertainers, including Johnny Ginger, Candy Johnson and longtime house band the Glen Covington Band.

The late Chester Devenow, a former titan of Toledo industry, said in 2002 that the Aku-Aku was "a gathering place for the top and bottom of society—the elite to the lowest characters that Toledo had to offer. It was the most important gathering place for the last generation of Toledo."

A souvenir lighter was distributed to patrons at the Aku-Aku Polynesian Room. *Courtesy of Greg Shapiro.*

Retired Toledo police detective Gene Fodor, who called the Aku-Aku "a jewel of a place," also noted that its clientele was a cross section of society, from politicians and businessmen to Detroit mobsters.

The man who brought the touch of Vegas to Toledo was Shapiro, whom one reporter described as a "Damon Runyan–type individual," referring to the famous American author's cast of colorful characters. Shapiro was a congenial host, who greeted his customers and worked hard to make it look like he wasn't working. "It helps guests relax and enjoy themselves more," he explained.

Shapiro grew up in Toledo's Old West End neighborhood, lived in Cleveland for a while and worked in Las Vegas, where he owned a cleaning-supply manufacturing business. His circle of celebrity friends included boxer Rocky Marciano, actor Joey Bishop and columnist Earl Wilson, as well as some reputed mobsters. Shapiro returned to Toledo and owned several restaurants, including the Embers Supper Club, Giuseppe's Italian Village, the Gas Light Club and Grenada Gardens, before opening the Aku-Aku.

The supper club and motel were designed in a modernistic '60s style of architecture known as Googie. The dining room advertised "Polynesian Food—a real treat—plus steaks, chops, and seafood," and a menu from the mid-1960s included a twenty-four-ounce porterhouse steak dinner for $6.95 and the evening special, a whole live Maine lobster dinner for $3.95.

The Polynesian-themed drinks included the "West Indies Sour," the "Aku-Aku Daiquiri" and the "Aku-Aku Gold Cup," made with Jamaican rum, "aged liquor," pineapple juice and limes for $1.25.

Seymour Rothman, a *Blade* columnist, said the Aku-Aku was "the action place to be in the '60s, the last of the great supper clubs." Noting its reputation for hosting racketeers, Rothman said the dining room included a curtained-off section "so that selected visitors could view the entertainment without being viewed themselves."

In 1965, the Town House Motel added a third story with thirty-one "penthouse suites" at a cost of $275,000. But when Shapiro left in 1970, the Aku-Aku stopped bringing in national acts, instead featuring local musicians. The hotel closed, and the building was sold at a sheriff's auction for $755,000 in 1972. The property changed hands several times after that with plans that included turning it into the "Truckers Inn 75," catering to truck drivers. It was demolished in 1989 and today is the site of a Rally's drive-through restaurant.

THE ASYLUM/CLUB BIJOU

When it comes to rock-and-roll, Toledoans can raise a toast to dozens of nightclubs that have come and gone. Most relied on local artists to draw crowds with an occasional national touring act taking the stage. But few, if any, Toledo venues of the past can compare to the steady, high-profile rock-and-roll lineup presented at the Asylum, later renamed Club Bijou, in its heyday.

"The Asylum definitely was legendary for a few years there," said Anthony Makes, a promoter who booked the shows with his business partner, Alberto Spallino. "We always talk about how mind-blowing it was with the talent we brought to the city and that venue in such a short time. It was wild," said Makes, who went on to a career in the concert promotion business.

The Esquire Theater closed in 1978 but was reopened in the 1990s as the Asylum, a music hot spot. *Toledo-Lucas County Public Library.*

The club at 209 North Superior Street originally opened in January 1941 as the Esquire Theater and featured everything from movies to vaudeville to burlesque over the decades before being bought by Toledo nightclub entrepreneur Kypros "Kip" Diacou in the early 1990s.

Diacou quickly renamed the club the Asylum and turned it into a rock-and-roll palace. The downtown venue had a large stage, an open floor area that could accommodate either tables and chairs or a standing-room crowd to suit the show, tables on several different tiers and two full-service bars.

"I loved that building!" said John Nittolo of Naples, Florida, who has been promoting concerts in Toledo for twenty years. "I put on thirty shows at the Asylum. Greg Allman was the first one I did there. It was an old vaudeville club, but I straight up loved it. It had general admission on the floor, seating on different levels, a bar on top and a bar on the bottom. Good dressing rooms underneath. It was just perfect."

The building had a separate, smaller room in the basement called the Underground, and during the mid-1990s, when Makes and Spallino were booking the shows, the Asylum often had two different concerts going on

The Asylum was renamed Club Bijou and then torn down to make way for the Huntington Center. The club's sign lies behind an uptown business. *Author's collection.*

at the same time—one thousand people upstairs in the theater and several hundred in the basement.

It was a favorite stop for musicians, who often made an effort to come back to the venue. Shock rocker Marilyn Manson, for one, played a sold-out concert at the Asylum in October 1995 and returned three months later for another sell-out on the same tour. The Verve Pipe, a Michigan band that topped the charts in 1997 with its hit single, "The Freshman," played at the Asylum in February and June of '97.

From 1995 to 1997, the Asylum and the Underground boasted a concert lineup that rivaled those of similar-sized clubs in New York or Los Angeles, presenting an eclectic mix of artists ranging from heavy metal to folk to blues. Among the bands and artists who played the venues were Marilyn Manson, Gavin DeGraw, Motörhead, Our Lady Peace, Big Head Todd and the Monsters, They Might Be Giants, the Jesus Lizard, Matthew Sweet, the Tragically Hip, Jackyl, Papa Roach, Zakk Wylde and James Cotton.

The Asylum, which in the late 1990s was renamed Club Bijou, was part of a city block that was demolished in 2007 to make way for a new eighty-thousand-seat arena, now called the Huntington Center. Diacou sold the nightclub to Lucas County for $2.3 million.

While music fans complained about the club's closing, they could not stop the wrecking ball. "I hated to lose that place because we brought in some fabulous shows in there," Nittolo, the concert promoter, said.

THE PEPPERMINT CLUB

Going back a few decades, one of the hottest places in Toledo for rock-and-roll was the Peppermint Club, on the corner of Jefferson Avenue and Ontario Street.

The club was originally Burt's Theater, a 1,500-seat opera house designed by famed Toledo architect George Mills that opened in 1898. It had an ornate stone-and-brick façade in a Venetian-Gothic design, with window balconies, a gentlemen's smoking room, a ladies' parlor and an extra-wide "fat man's row," according to Toledo historian William D. Speck.

Burt sold the building in 1908, and it reopened as the American Music Theater in 1909. In 1916, the building was remodeled into an auto showroom and later into a warehouse.

In 1962, Duane Abbajay, a twenty-nine-year-old construction company owner, took over the business of running the Peppermint Club from his

Burt's Theater, a 1,500-seat opera house, opened on Jefferson Avenue at Ontario Street in 1898. It was reborn as the Peppermint Club in the 1960s. *Author's collection.*

brother Donny, who was facing financial disaster. Abbajay renovated the building's main music area and began bringing in some of the nation's most famous, chart-topping rock-and-rollers. From the early to mid-'60s, many legendary names in rock history performed at the Peppermint Club, including Jerry Lee Lewis, the Everly Brothers, Fats Domino, Chubby Checker and the Four Seasons.

In 1964, Lewis, who performed at the Peppermint Club at least four times in the mid-'60s, brought along a then unknown singer from Wales named Tom Jones. According to an article by Abbajay's daughter Stephanie Abbajay, the two performers had met in Chicago and were both heading to Detroit when Lewis offered Jones a ride. They stopped in Toledo because Lewis was scheduled to play a show at the Peppermint Club. Jones, never shy about his talents, asked Abbajay if he could sing a few songs that night, but when Abbajay heard the singer's "funny accent and took in Jones's frilly shirt, long curly hair and tight black pants," he turned him down. The club owner actually feared for Jones's safety amid the blue-collar Toledo crowd, according to the daughter, and advised the

Welshman to sit quietly in a corner until Lewis was done performing. A year later, Jones became world famous when his song "It's Not Unusual" topped the singles charts.

Tommy James, leader of the '60s rock band the Shondells, said he and his friends often drove to Toledo from their hometown of Niles, Michigan—about two and a half hours away—to go to the Peppermint Lounge for the music and the beer. In Michigan at the time, James said, anyone under twenty-one could not drink regular beer, only beer with an alcohol content of less than 3.2 percent. Ohio's alcohol laws were more lenient toward teens, and that made it worth the drive, according to James.

Abbajay was a "pioneer impresario of American rock-and-roll, at least in Toledo." He did most of his business upstairs in the club's office, where his desk was piled with papers and the shelves were stocked with cash, candy, tequila bottles and a loaded pistol. Abbajay owned the nightclub for nearly thirty years, including a time in the 1970s when he renamed it the Country Palace, taking advantage of the surging popularity of country music.

Legend has it that Kenny Rogers's hit song "Lucille," which opens with the line "In a bar in Toledo, across from the depot," was inspired by a conversation overheard at the Peppermint Club. Hal Bynum, who co-wrote the song with Rogers, told the *Blade* that he came to Toledo by bus in the summer of 1975, walked across the street from the Greyhound station and went inside the Peppermint Club for a drink. A couple seated nearby got into a heated argument, and the man stood up to leave and told the woman, "All I can say is, you picked a fine time to leave me." Bynum added the name Lucille to make the lyrics rhyme, and the song became Rogers's first number-one hit in 1977. Rogers, however, offered a different version of how the song came about. He told talk show host Dinah Shore on her show in 1977 that he heard a man deliver that famous parting line, word for word, while watching a local news program in Oklahoma.

When Kenny Rogers played at the Toledo Sports Arena, he made a detour to the Country Palace and gave Abbajay a signed copy of a "Lucille" record. He also put his hands and feet in a block of cement, but in a strange twist, his shoes got stuck in the concrete, and he "left the club in his stocking feet," according to Stephanie Abbajay.

The Peppermint Club had a number of other names after Abbajay sold it in 1989, most notably Caesar's Show Bar, a venue where female impersonators, including the 825-pound Odessa Brown, performed drag shows in the 1990s. The building has been vacant since 2010.

8
THE TOLEDO SPORTS ARENA

HOCKEY, STARS AND ELEPHANTS

The Toledo Sports Arena wasn't much to look at, but for six decades, the plain but functional building fondly called "the Old Barn" was home to many of the city's biggest moments in sports and entertainment.

Built at a cost of $1 million, the twenty-thousand-square-foot arena opened its doors on December 13, 1947, as the new home ice for Toledo's professional minor-league hockey team, the Mercurys. The Mercs played at the arena for the next fifteen years (renamed the Buckeyes for one season, 1949–50) and were followed by a succession of minor-league teams: the Blades (1963–68), the Hornets (1970–74), the Goaldiggers (1974–86) and the Storm (1991–2007).

The boxy brick-and-concrete arena was designed as a multipurpose building, with 5,230 fixed seats and the ability to accommodate 8,000 when the main floor was opened up to spectators. The building had enough flexibility to adapt to just about any athletic event, hosting boxing, wrestling, basketball, bowling, soccer, swimming, gymnastics, lacrosse, rodeos, monster trucks, roller derbies and "toughman" contests.

Family events were held regularly in the arena, including open skating nights, Harlem Globetrotters exhibition games, Disney on Ice, Sesame Street Live and circuses, including the Shrine Circus, the Royal Hanneford and the Ringling Bros. & Barnum and Bailey Circus (the arena's low ceiling forced Ringling Bros. to forgo its popular human cannonball act). And it also hosted some not-so-family-oriented events, particularly two male revues, including one by the Chippendales, in the late 1980s.

The Toledo Sports Arena is visible to the right of the bridge on the near side of the Maumee River. *Toledo–Lucas County Public Library.*

The Toledo Sports Arena was a sports and entertainment mecca from 1947 until 2007. *Toledo–Lucas County Public Library.*

In 1947 and 1948, the arena was home court for the Toledo Jeeps, a short-lived pro basketball franchise that played in the National Basketball League.

In 1949, entertainment icon Bob Hope performed a USO show at the Sports Arena featuring a forty-member troupe, including actresses Doris

The Shrine Circus, shown here in the 1960s, was one of the many family-friendly entertainment events presented at the Toledo Sports Arena. *Toledo–Lucas County Public Library.*

Day and Irene Ryan. In February of that year, cowboy star Gene Autry performed a variety show at the Sports Arena with musical guests and rode his famous horse, Champion, down the aisle, pausing to let fans pet the animal.

In 1952, light heavyweight boxer Archie Moore fought Harold Johnson before a crowd of eight thousand.

In 1959, seventeen-year-old Cassius Clay won five fights in an AAU tournament at the Sports Arena, one year before turning pro and becoming the most famous boxer in history (changing his name to Muhammad Ali in 1964).

In 1960, the American Bowling Congress held a tournament in the Toledo Sports Arena that lasted six months, with thirty-six bowling lanes set up in a thirty-thousand-square foot exhibit hall that had just been added on to the facility.

The NBA's Detroit Pistons played three "home games" at the Sports Arena during the 1962–63 season, but virtually all the players said the arena's portable basketball floor was the worst surface they had ever played on.

Rubin "Hurricane" Carter, the boxer immortalized in a Bob Dylan song and a Hollywood movie, fought Toledo's Wilbert "Skeeter" McClure to a draw in the venue in 1966.

In 1980, two people were shot to death in the Sports Arena during a closed-circuit broadcast of the Sugar Ray Leonard–Roberto Duran boxing match.

The Toledo Pride soccer team played just one season, 1986–87, in the American Indoor Soccer Association, on a field of AstroTurf laid on top of the Sports Arena's cement floor. The team drew an average of 1,700 per game and finished with fourteen wins and twenty-eight losses.

Wrestler Hulk Hogan drew a capacity crowd of 8,251 when he was the star of a World Wrestling Federation event at the arena on December 26, 1987.

For an Aqua Parade in 1949, the floor of the arena was filled with a giant swimming pool. For the Coors Light Motor Spectacular in 1987, a pit on the arena floor was filled with one hundred dump-truck loads of dirt and ten thousand gallons of water.

Former general manager Andy Mulligan once said, "Everything has been held here except a national convention of hoboes."

Unlike the ornate movie and entertainment theaters in downtown Toledo that were adorned with crystal chandeliers, plush carpets and velvet curtains, the Sports Arena was bunker-like in its design, devoid of all decorative flourishes. Concrete was the dominant theme, from the arena floor (when it wasn't covered by ice) to its cramped hallways, which were painted an institutional beige and white. Many of the pillars in the building featured hand-painted warnings in big block letters: "WATCH OUT FOR FLYING PUCKS."

Hockey was the main reason that Toledo businessmen Virgil Gladieux and Emery Gilbert joined forces to build a facility larger than the 2,600-seat Ice House on Berdan Avenue. They searched for a site in the heart of downtown but ended up building the Sports Arena on eighteen acres at One Main Street in East Toledo, across the Maumee River from downtown at the foot of the Cherry Street Bridge.

Toledo's minor-league teams won eleven hockey championships in sixty years of competing at the Sports Arena. Fans loved the building because the seats were all within forty feet of the ice. Opponents hated to play in Toledo because the arena was loud and the sound echoed. And Toledo hockey fans had a habit of throwing chairs at opponents or squirting them with ketchup or mustard. Toledo hockey lovers were at their worst when the arena held its popular ten-cent beer nights.

Nick Vitucci was the "old man" of the Toledo Storm hockey team. *Toledo–Lucas County Public Library.*

Mike Eruzione, captain of the U.S. 1980 Olympic Gold Medal hockey team, played two seasons as a forward for the Toledo Goaldiggers, winning the International Hockey League's Rookie of the Year Award in 1978 and leading the team to the Turner Cup championship that season.

Nick Vitucci, one of the Toledo Storm's coaches, said the arena, known as the "Old Barn," was a great place for the home team. "The atmosphere was second to none. The enthusiasm and loudness [were] deafening," he said.

For rock concerts, the Sports Arena had a stage that was big enough for most touring bands, measuring forty feet deep by fifty-six feet wide. But the amenities were primitive for performers and spectators alike—especially when compared to the luxuries of modern arenas.

When Bad Company came to town at the height of its popularity in 1975, for example, the band members flew into Toledo on a private jet dubbed the "Bad Ship" and were driven to the Sports Arena in stretch Cadillac limousines. After such a lofty arrival, the rock stars were rudely brought down to earth by the harsh realities of the Sports Arena's bare-bones backstage. Guitarist Mick Ralphs had to tune his dozen or so guitars in a closed-off men's room, laying his electric Gibson and Fender instruments on folding tables with their headstocks hovering just inches above the urinals.

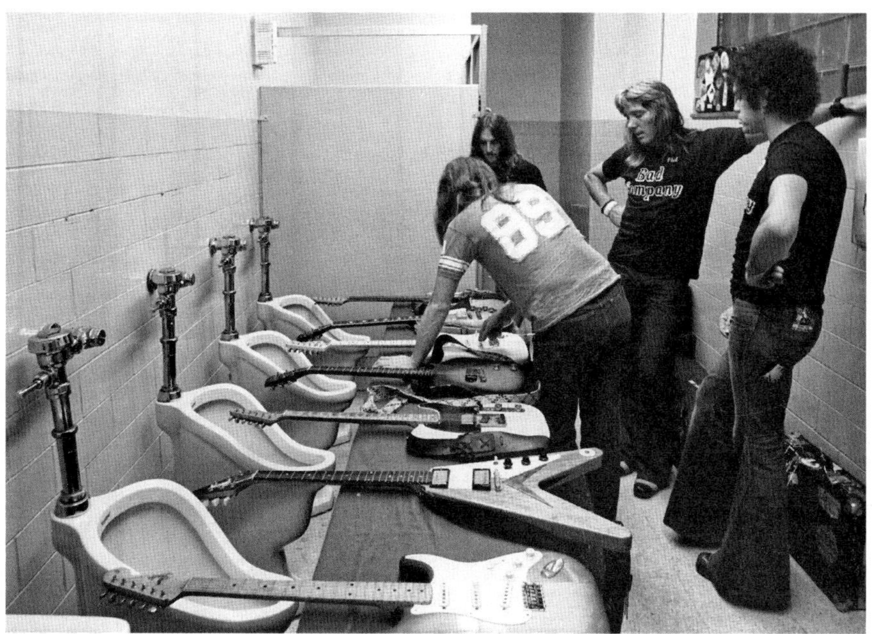

Mick Ralphs of Bad Company (in jersey No. 89) inspects his guitars in the Sports Arena's unglamorous backstage. *Courtesy of John Gibbs Rockwood.*

Bad Company's May 21, 1975 show at the Toledo Sports Arena was featured prominently in a *Rolling Stone* magazine article published on July 3, 1975, written by famed rock critic Chet Flippo, who had followed the band on tour. Among other things, Flippo called the Sports Arena "a confining, poorly ventilated hall." He quoted lead singer Paul Rodgers, saying the Toledo show "wasn't good" because "the air was too hot. The air was so heavy the crowd was just down." He added that Rodgers was in a "foul mood" before arriving in Toledo, having fractured his left hand earlier in the day in "an encounter with a door."

Although the arena's backstage amenities were spartan, and the hockey team's locker room was the size of a closet, the indoor space behind the stage was cavernous. It was big enough to keep circus elephants comfortable and to park a dozen tour buses if necessary. The rock bands preferred to hang out in the vast expanses behind the stage rather than in the arena's tiny locker rooms, using curtained-off "rooms" divided by movable posts.

Stephen Hartzell of Tiffin, Ohio, who writes a blog about northwest Ohio history, reminisced about the many times he made the fifty-five-mile trip to Toledo for a concert at the Sports Arena:

Greg Allman performs in concert in the 1980s at the Toledo Sports Arena. *Courtesy of John Gibbs Rockwood.*

> *Back in the '70s, a typical concert experience began weeks before the event as we stood in line at Finders Records to buy our tickets, which were all general admission and cost about six dollars each. On the day of the event, a friend with a large car or van began to round up his friends to make the trip to Toledo… Throughout the trip, adult beverages and other supplies were liberally partaken of…The sight of our gang spilling out of the vehicle would surely have been a comical one, were it not for the fact that it was so very commonplace at the time.*

Fans who were intent on getting close to the stage arrived early and lined up outside the front entrance, waiting for the doors to open. Police and security guards would give them "a long look," Hartzell said, "but once you were in, you were free to drink and smoke whatever you brought with you. And people did, like crazy." When the lights dimmed and the concert began, the arena would fill up with smoke, Hartzell recalled, mostly from cigarettes but also from "cigarettes of the less-than-legal variety."

The roster of bands and artists who played at the Toledo Sports Arena reads like a who's who in rock history. Here are some of the notable names who appeared at the venue:

- **1950s**: Elvis Presley, Johnny Cash, Dean Martin and Jerry Lewis, Frankie Lymon and the Teenagers, Duke Ellington Orchestra with Sarah Vaughan and Nat King Cole.
- **1960s**: The Beach Boys, Paul Revere & the Raiders, Tommy James & the Shondells, Neil Diamond, the Amboy Dukes, Three Dog Night, Steppenwolf and the MC5.
- **1970s**: Bob Seger, David Bowie, KISS, Bruce Springsteen and the E Street Band, Bad Company, the Cars, Fleetwood Mac, Rod Stewart and the Faces, Mott the Hoople, Uriah Heep, Greg Allman, Mitch Ryder, Chicago, the Mahavishnu Orchestra, Queen, Santana, Foghat, Frank Zappa, Heart, Buddy Guy and Muddy Waters, Blue Oyster Cult, Van Halen, Grand Funk and Eric Burdon, Jethro Tull, Parliament/Funkadelic, Humble Pie, Leon Russell, Slade and the James Gang, Robin Trower, Iggy and the Stooges, Alice Cooper, Mountain, Johnny Winter, UFO, Styx, Joe Walsh, Dr. John, the J. Geils Band and Peter Frampton, Golden Earring, Electric Light Orchestra, the Doobie Brothers and Brownsville Station.
- **1980s**: Metallica, Black Sabbath, Guns N' Roses, Scorpions and Iron Maiden, Whitesnake, AC/DC, Nazareth, Rush, Ratt, Dio, Eddie Money, Molly Hatchett, ZZ Top, Def Leppard, Deep Purple, Mahogany Rush with Angel and Humble Pie, Thin Lizzy and Journey, Cheap Trick, Sammy Hagar, David Lee Roth, Beastie Boys, Run DMC and LL Cool J and Yngwie Malmsteen.
- **1990s**: Kid Rock, Alanis Morissette, Nine Inch Nails, Tesla, Tool, the Cult, Poison, Slaughter, Bonham, Cinderella, Judas Priest, Dokken, Mötley Crüe and Ozzy Osbourne.

Elvis Presley performed two thirty-minute shows at the Sports Arena on Thanksgiving Day 1956—the matinee and evening shows drawing a total of 13,125 fans. Tickets cost from $2.00 to $2.50 and were still available the day before the show, according to advertisements. Presley's Sports Arena appearance came in a year when his career was on a meteoric rise with a string of hits that included "Love Me Tender," "Hound Dog," "Don't Be Cruel," "Heartbreak Hotel," "All Shook Up" and "Blue Suede Shoes."

"In the space of a year," the *Blade* concert review noted, "Presley has soared from a $35 a week truck driver in Memphis, Tenn., to a singing sensation who can take home better than $16,000 for a one-day stand in Toledo."

The reviewer did not try to mask his skepticism of Presley's talent. He wrote that the warm-up act *suddenly whipped the tempo into the pulsating rock and roll rhythm that Elvis has made his specialty. The tension mounted until he appeared at the rear of the stage. Presley stumbled forward, looked about in an almost bewildered amazement and launched into his first number. It brought the house down. From the opening chord, nothing could be heard but a steady, high-pitched scream, pierced occasionally by pleas of "Over here, Elvis…"*

Elvis Presley boasts he has never had a music lesson, an educational void he clearly demonstrated when he performed. But it made no difference. The all-but-hysterical screams that accompanied his every number completely

Elvis Presley played Toledo twice: the Sports Arena in 1956 and, shown here, the University of Toledo in 1977. *Courtesy of John Gibbs Rockwood.*

> *obliterated whatever sounds he was making vocally, or might have made on his standard prop—a huge guitar that he strums from time to time but never plays.*

When Presley walked off the stage, the crowd surged past the twenty policemen who were hired to guard the stage. But Elvis had already left the building. He was driven to the Commodore Perry Hotel downtown, where he took a seat in the Shalimar Room with his press agent and three musicians. A nineteen-year-old Toledo man suddenly confronted Presley, shouting, "My wife carries your picture but doesn't carry mine!" A free-for-all ensued, and police arrived to find Presley pummeling the accuser. The brawl was later revealed to have been a publicity stunt.

Presley returned to Toledo just one other time, for a concert at the University of Toledo's Centennial Hall on April 25, 1977. As with his first Toledo visit, the newspaper was not exactly kind. Reviewer Greg Oatis described the legendary entertainer as "a pudgy, middle-aged man whose mumbled lyrics and feeble attempts at pelvis thrusts were a parody [of his former self]." Angry fans wrote letters to the editor and called to complain about the harsh words. Less than four months later, Presley died at his Graceland mansion at age forty-two.

Singer-showman Alice Cooper played a show in Toledo in December 1973 that ended in a riot. During the first song, a fan threw something at the singer—reportedly an egg—and hit Cooper in the shoulder. The singer carried on with the show for a few more minutes until an M-80 firework exploded in the rafters, shattering some lights and sending glass cascading down onto the band. Cooper immediately left the stage and didn't come back. When an announcement was made over the PA that the show was over, outraged fans started a riot. Police in riot gear were called to the scene and restored order.

One regular visitor to the Toledo Sports Arena was Ted Nugent, the Motor City Madman, who played there from the 1960s when he was in the Amboy Dukes until the 1990s. He also made the Sports Arena an annual stop on his "Whiplash Bash," an end-of-the-year mini-tour that stayed close to his hometown of Detroit. When Nugent played the Sports Arena with his all-star band the Damn Yankees in December 1992, some fans flew to Toledo from Germany to see their rock hero in concert. "If the Damn Yankees won't come to us, we must come to the Damn Yankees," one of the German tourists stated.

The notorious bad boy Axl Rose led Guns N' Roses in concert at Toledo Sports Arena on May 1, 1988, in a show that has been preserved for posterity as a popular "bootleg" DVD set (recorded and sold illegally).

KISS fans pack the Toledo Sports Arena for a concert in the 1970s. *Courtesy of John Gibbs Rockwood.*

A memorable moment in arena lore occurred on November 28, 1981, when the electricity went out about fifteen minutes into a show by heavy metal band Black Sabbath. Battery-powered emergency lights clicked on, providing minimal lighting, and power was restored after forty-five minutes. Arena officials praised the crowd of 3,700 for enduring the Black Sabbath blackout without incident.

Beyond dispute, the hottest show in Toledo Sports Arena history goes to British prog-rock band Yes. When the group played a concert on July 30, 1977, the temperature inside the building reached a precipitous 126 degrees, drummer Alan White recalled. The memory of that sauna-like setting provided the inspiration for Yes to prominently mention Toledo in its 1983 tune "Our Song." "It was the hottest gig we ever played," White said. "I remember it was so hot that when I got off stage I had lost so much water that I had an inch of sweat inside my tennis shoes."

Liquids also tended to puddle on top of the arena's cement floor, where rock fans often sloshed around in a thin lake of spilled beer. When folding chairs were set up on the main floor, Hartzell said the rows were spaced far enough apart that people could stand up and walk to an aisle without hindrance. Such generous spacing is not to be found in the Sports Arena's successor, the $105 million Huntington Center. The multipurpose facility opened in 2009 in downtown Toledo and accommodates up to eight thousand people, but fans must squeeze their way to and from the floor seats, Hartzell noted after attending a Bob Seger concert in 2015. "The seats in front of us were less than two inches in front of my knees," he said. "In order to let someone out, you had to stand up and fold up your seat."

The atmosphere of rock concerts at the Sports Arena from the '70s and '80s just can't be duplicated, Hartzell said. "The pure energy that passed between the artists and the audience was often both intense and at once indescribable. This was a generation that shared an unprecedented love affair with their music, and with the artists who created it."

The last big rock show at the Toledo Sports Arena was the "Get Out the Vote" concert promoting Democrat John Kerry's bid for the White House. The all-star lineup that played in Toledo on October 2, 2004, featured grunge rock supergroup Pearl Jam, with opening act Death Cab for Cutie. Special guests Neil Young, Peter Frampton and actor Tim Robbins made unannounced appearances that night. Pearl Jam's lead singer Eddie Vedder also made an unannounced visit, stepping outside the building before the show and chatting with fans about politics. When one person asked Vedder for an autograph, the singer replied, "Whoa, first let's talk about the election."

The sports arena's swan song was an "extreme toughman contest," similar to the Ultimate Fighting Championship, held on April 28, 2007.

Four months later, demolition began with a swing of the sledgehammer by Toledo mayor Carty Finkbeiner, who bashed a wall at the back of the building. A crowd of about 150 people gathered around the building for the ceremony. Wearing a hard hat, Finkbeiner told onlookers that the Sports Arena had brought much joy, happiness and excitement over the decades, but for the tens of thousands of Toledoans who attended events in the building, their memories will live forever.

"When the Sports Arena was torn down," Hartzell said, "I knew that there would never be another venue quite like it again. The page was turned."

9

TOLEDO WHEELS

BICYCLES, AUTOS AND JEEPS

Toledo's location on the Maumee River—the largest river draining into Lake Erie—led the way for the port city to become a transportation hub during America's westward expansion.

In the second half of the 1800s, the growth of America's canals, railroads and roadways continued to strengthen Toledo's role as a major crossroads.

One of the classic Jeep models, this one from 1955, manufactured by Toledo's Willys-Overland Motor Co. *Toledo–Lucas County Public Library.*

The city's businesses were thriving, and the population was growing rapidly. That boomtown environment drew scores of newcomers looking to begin a new life and dreaming of making their fortunes. Toledo's population grew from 1,200 in 1840 to 31,600 in 1870 and 131,800 by the end of the century.

As Henry Ford was helping Detroit's transformation into the Motor City, Toledo's proximity to the center of the nation's auto industry made it a logical place for spinoff businesses, from companies competing to build new vehicles to those supplying parts, from starters to windshields, for the big automakers.

The Jeep was first mass produced in Toledo as a military vehicle for use in World War II, and thousands of Toledoans have been assembling Jeeps ever since. Corporate ownership of the brand has changed over the decades, but the enduring popularity of Jeeps has made the vehicles' name and heritage synonymous with the city.

Toledo's connection to the auto industry, however, goes back long before the first Jeep rolled off the assembly line in 1941. The city's involvement in the auto industry started more than 140 years ago, with the arrival of the Milburn Wagon Works in 1873.

A group of Toledo business leaders persuaded George Milburn, president of one of the nation's largest wagon makers, to relocate his factory from Mishawaka, Indiana, where it was founded in 1858. The move came after Milburn's request to extend a rail line to the Mishawaka factory was denied. Compounding the wagon maker's struggles, the plant in Indiana was having difficulty getting enough lumber to meet its production needs. The Toledo businessmen raised $300,000 to entice Milburn to move and pledged the city's full cooperation in obtaining suitable property and rail service. They pointed out that Toledo had five lumber mills, dozens of lumber agents and dealers and processed millions of feet of Ohio and Michigan lumber annually.

When Milburn moved his company to Toledo in 1873, he brought the entire company with him—not just the equipment, but the factory workers as well.

Toledo partially financed construction of the Milburn Wagon Works on a thirty-two-acre site at 3134 Monroe Street, two miles from downtown in the city's new Auburndale neighborhood. A rail line was built to accommodate the manufacturer, with the line extending half a mile beyond the wagon works. Milburn erected two principal buildings, each 365 feet long, 80 feet wide and five stories high.

In 1876, journalist Richard Edwards lauded the appearance of the new factory in an article published in *Historical and Business Review*:

> *On approaching the works from the city side one is struck particularly with the great taste shown in the architectural design of the buildings; builders of factories usually seem to consider themselves under some sort of obligation to render them as unsightly and comfortless looking as aggregations of brick and mortar can be made...The managers of the wagon works deserve the thanks of the entire community for the liberal taste they have shown in the designs for these buildings.*

When the plant began production in 1875, it employed 150 men and produced sixty-five different types of wagons. Its specialty was wagons used in farming, with the capacities to carry between one thousand and twelve thousand pounds. But Milburn also made specialty wagons for a wide range of purposes, including the delivery of mail, ice, meat, candy, oil, baked goods and beer. It manufactured lance wagons used for carrying poles, garbage wagons for hauling waste and ambulances for medical transport. The new Toledo factory could produce as many as 20,000 wagons a year, although Edwards reported that 4,121 were manufactured in the first half of 1876, for an average of about 30 per day.

The plant was fully mechanized, with men guiding machines that created every part of the wagon, from the wooden frames to the iron wheels. The wagon works annually used 150,000 feet of ash, 250,000 feet of hickory, 100,000 feet of elm, 1.5 million feet of pine and whitewood, 4 million tons of iron and steel and 200,000 pounds of paint.

George Milburn sold his interest in Milburn Wagon Works in 1880, due to failing health. He retired in Kansas, where he died in 1883 at age sixty-two.

The company's rapid growth continued, however, and by the mid-1880s, Milburn claimed to be the world's largest wagon manufacturer.

Around 1910, the company began producing bodies for the Ohio Electric car, as well as supplying bodies for gasoline-powered cars that were being manufactured by firms such as Ford, Ohio Electric, Willys, Overland and Oldsmobile. The company made lofty promises for its cars, as evidenced in a 1915 advertisement in *Literary Digest* asserting that the Ohio Electric "is built with but one goal in view—perfection."

> *It is intended solely for those who will have nothing else. Its appeal is not to individuals who can, or must, be satisfied with less. Perfection is not a matter of dollars-and-cents measurement. As well might Raphael have tried to save a tube of pigment in painting the Madonna; or Michael Angelo a few hours' labor in carving a masterpiece. Therefore, time or skill*

> *or money have not been spared in producing the Ohio Electric. And its price is in fair accordance with the marvelous artistic achievement it embodies.*

In September 1914, the wagon maker began manufacturing its own line of electric cars, the Milburn Light Electric. Over the next eight years, it built four thousand cars that sold for between $1,285 and $1,485 each. The 1915 Milburn had four forward speeds and two reverse speeds, a range of fifty miles on a charge and a top speed of nineteen miles per hour.

The cars, which were considered among the most elegant and reliable of the era, were used by Secret Service agents, and President Woodrow Wilson owned a 1918 Milburn Electric that he personally drove around the White House grounds.

By 1921, Milburn was employing eight hundred workers in manufacturing its own line of electric cars, taxicabs and trucks, as well as automobile bodies for other automakers.

In February 1923, Milburn Wagon Works was purchased by General Motors for $2 million, as the Detroit automaker sought a quick solution to meet the growing demand for its vehicles. Today, the former Milburn plant is the site of a Wendy's restaurant and a four-story office building for the Lucas County Department of Jobs and Family Services. At least fifty Milburn Electric vehicles are still in existence.

Just as Milburn Wagon Works made the transition to automating, so did Toledo's first bicycle manufacturer, the Lozier and Yost Bicycle Works.

Joseph L. Yost, treasurer and manager of the Springfield (Massachusetts) Bicycle Company, relocated his firm to Toledo in 1889, moving into a factory on Central Avenue, just west of Detroit Avenue, previously owned by the former Jewel Manufacturing Company, which manufactured sewing machines, marine motors and bicycles. Yost, who in addition to his business role served two terms as Lucas County treasurer, was in the vanguard of Toledo's burgeoning bicycle industry.

The local bicycle industry flourished with the development of the "safety bicycle," which was lightweight, propelled by pedals and had two equal-sized tires. Previous versions of the bicycle had a large front wheel, were difficult to pedal and often plunged forward when they struck an obstacle.

In 1898, there were twenty-two bicycle manufacturers and nine bicycle-parts suppliers in Toledo, and the city was compared to Coventry, England, the center of Europe's bicycle-manufacturing industry. In an 1896 article, the *Blade* asserted that "Toledo is the Coventry of America and the most prosperous and thriving city in the United States."

Unlike modern society's use of bicycles as either a leisure activity or a machine made for exercise, in the late 1800s, the bicycle was considered an important and revolutionary means of transportation.

George K. Detwiler, a prominent real estate developer, stated in 1895 that bicycles had changed the dynamics of home ownership: "The [bicycle] annihilates distance and people are willing to get away from the rush and bustle of the center of the city. It has also increased the sale of outside property, for many have bought homes two and three miles distant from the post office, who, if it were not for the wheel, would not be able to own a home at all."

In 1899, George Burwell, superintendent of the Lozier Bicycle Factory, collaborated with John Perrin to design a three-wheel, gasoline-powered car, and in 1900, Lozier became the first Toledoan to patent an automobile part with the invention of the engine cylinder lubricator.

Lozier moved his factory to New York State, and the building and equipment were purchased by the nation's largest bicycle manufacturer, American Bicycle Company, owned by Connecticut industrialist Albert A. Pope. By December 1900, Pope was building steam-powered, two-seat automobiles using such bicycle innovations as spoke wheels and tube frames.

Another Toledo bicycle magnate who entered the automating field was Peter Gendron, who, in September 1899, produced the second gas-powered car to be driven in Toledo. With a four-story factory at Superior and Orange Streets, Gendron became an innovator in the manufacture and application of bicycle components. He modified the production of wire spoke wheels and friction-reducing ball bearings to be used in making bicycles, baby carriages, wheelchairs and toy wagons.

In June 1902, it was reported that Toledo residents owned eighty-eight automobiles, making it one of the leading cities of its size in percentage of automobile ownership.

Some Toledoans who had been concerned by the rising popularity of automobiles proposed an ordinance to limit the speed of automobiles in the city limits to six miles per hour. After a second reading, however, the proposal was rejected as "inoperative and useless." Seven months later, in May 1902, a girl riding a bicycle was struck and killed by an automobile, becoming one of Toledo's first automobile fatalities.

The ABC bicycle maker was renamed the International Motor Car Company in 1902 and, in addition to building steam-powered vehicles, began making gasoline-driven automobiles with internal-combustion engines. The company's first luxury roadster, named the Pope-Toledo, sold for $3,000—more than most Toledoans earned in a year.

Despite its high price, the Pope-Toledo sold well for five years and garnered attention as one of the top race cars in the country. The Toledo won fifteen auto races in 1903 and thirty-three in 1904. On July 25, 1903, Arthur Moses, driving a twenty-four-horsepower Pope-Toledo, became the first person to drive a gas-powered automobile to the top of Mount Washington, New Hampshire—at 6,288 feet the highest peak east of the Mississippi River.

A number of fledgling companies in the Toledo area entered the auto-making business as the popularity of "horseless carriages" continued to rise in the early 1900s:

- The Elmore Manufacturing Company, founded in Clyde, Ohio, in 1893, produced several models of the Elmore automobile, with two-stroke engines in one, two and three cylinders. In 1908, the company was bought by William C. Durant, founder of General Motors.
- The Snell Fittings Company and the Kirk Manufacturing Company of Toledo jointly produced the Yale automobile in 1903 and 1904.
- The Craig-Toledo Company of Dundee, Michigan, in 1906 produced a gas-powered car called the Maumee.
- The De Luxe Motor Car Company of Toledo produced the De Luxe car in 1906 and 1907.
- The Belmont Motor Company of Toledo manufactured the Belmont Six in 1917.
- The Cyclomobile Manufacturing Company, Toledo, produced two lightweight models with air-cooled engines in 1920 and 1921.

When another successful bicycle manufacturer, John North Willys (pronounced WILL-is), entered the auto-making field, it had the greatest long-term impact on Toledo's role in the automotive industry, including the development of the city's most iconic vehicle, the Jeep.

Willys was born in Canandaigua, New York, in 1873 and began selling bicycles as a young man. Within a few years, he began manufacturing his own line of bicycles, and by 1900, at age twenty-seven, the company had annual sales of $500,000.

He saw his first automobile while visiting Cleveland in 1899 and noted how the vehicle drew the interest of every person who watched it go by. He correctly foresaw that the automobile would replace horses and bicycles and reshape American society. Willys returned to New York and opened an automobile dealership. After several lean years (selling a total of two cars in 1900 and 1901) he found success selling automobiles manufactured by Overland Motor

Company in Indianapolis. A problem arose when Willys began selling the cars faster than the factory in Indianapolis could supply them.

To investigate the situation, Willys visited the factory and found that it was shut down and that forty-five cars were sitting unfinished on the assembly line. He personally raised the funds needed for the automaker to resume production, and in 1908, Willys purchased the entire Overland Motors Company.

He moved the company to Toledo in 1911, purchasing the former Pope-Toledo factory for $285,000 and, in 1912, renaming it the Willys-Overland Motor Company.

Willys-Overland was producing 150,000 automobiles by 1915, the second-highest number in the United States behind Ford. Its mid-priced Willys-Knight, introduced in 1914, was one of the nation's best-selling cars, with approximately 50,000 sold each year from 1915 to 1940.

In 1915, the Toledo automaker built a seven-story headquarters near the factory, the largest single-tenant office building in Ohio at the time. The 160,000-square-foot building had four passenger elevators, one freight elevator, a cafeteria and an eight-hundred-seat auditorium. Willys's private, wood-paneled office was equipped with two telephone lines and a wood-burning fireplace.

By 1916, Willys-Overland employed seventeen thousand workers—one of every five wage earners in Toledo. Within two years, the factory spanned more than 4.4 million square feet, the equivalent of 103 acres, making it the largest single automobile plant in the world.

In 1925, the automaker's $27 million payroll equaled 41 percent of all the wages earned by Toledo workers. The peak employment year was 1928, when twenty-three thousand people worked in the 7-million-square-foot plant, which had ninety buildings on the 119-acre site.

Willys-Overland continued to flourish through most of the 1920s. When the company introduced the Whippet Six coach in May 1926, it was the smallest four-cylinder car on the market, and its sticker price of $695 made it an immediate sensation.

The company reached its production peak in 1928, when it sold 314,437 cars and earned a profit of $187 million. As the company was enjoying a boom year in 1929, John North Willys abruptly resigned as president—retaining his title as chairman of the board—and sold his common stock for a reported $25 million just before the onset of the Great Depression in October.

After Herbert Hoover became president in March 1929, Willys was appointed the U.S. ambassador to Poland, a position he served from 1930 until 1932. Willys died of a heart attack in 1935, at age sixty-one.

Spark plug manufacturer Champion moved from Boston to Toledo in 1910 to be close to the Willys-Overland plant. *Toledo–Lucas County Public Library.*

Among the Toledo companies that became known for making automobile parts were Champion, which manufactured spark plugs; Auto-Lite, which produced batteries, electric starters, ignition coils, spark plugs and other car parts; and Spicer, which is credited with developing the four-wheel drive used in Jeeps.

Champion was founded in Boston in 1908 by brothers Robert A. Stranahan and Frank D. Stranahan, who decided to move to Toledo in 1910 to be close to Willys-Overland, then the country's number-two automaker. The Stranahans quickly signed contracts with Willys-Overland and with Ford Motor Co., and within two years, Champion had become the world's largest spark plug manufacturer.

Still a world leader in the manufacture of spark plugs, Champion was sold for $700 million to Cooper Industries in 1989 and shortly after moved its operations out of Toledo.

Historic Labor Strike

Toledo's Auto-Lite plant, on Champlain Street on the edge of downtown, was the scene of one of the most important labor strikes in U.S. history. The strike occurred at a time when court rulings made the legal status of labor unions uncertain, and the economy was in turmoil from the Great Depression. Unemployment among Toledo industrial workers was as high as 80 percent, and company officials often reminded workers that there were lines of people ready to take their jobs.

When Auto-Lite workers voted in February 1934 to organize as part of the Federal Labor Unions Local 18384, the company agreed to acknowledge the union's existence. At the same time, Auto-Lite's owners refused to recognize the union as a bargaining agent for the workers.

Workers went on strike on April 12 and began picketing the factory on Friday, April 13. The strike had little impact, however, as half the factory workers crossed the picket lines, and Auto-Lite hired scores of replacement workers. Tensions increased daily, and there was sporadic violence, including strikebreakers being hit by flying bricks. One replacement worker who went to the factory to pick up his paycheck was grabbed by the protesters, stripped down to just his shoes and a necktie and paraded through the streets until rescued by police. On May 15, sheriff's deputies arrested 107 demonstrators, and 46 more the following day.

On May 23, a crowd of approximately six thousand rallied outside the factory, and when someone threw a heavy steel bracket from the building, hitting female picketer Alma Hahn in the neck and ear, the demonstrators stormed the building, only to be dispersed by tear gas.

The strike quickly became a rallying point for Toledoans who were struggling through the Great Depression. Thousands more showed up the next day, surrounding the Auto-Lite building, trapping the workers inside and keeping others from entering. They threw rocks and bricks, breaking every window in the building.

The Ohio National Guard was called in, with nine hundred guardsmen arriving at 4:30 a.m. on May 24. They drove back the crowd, set up machine-gun posts at street corners near the plant and by 7:30 a.m. had cleared the way for workers inside the plant to leave, escorted out by the busload.

The next day, May 24, a full-scale battle erupted between the protesters and the National Guard, with the crowd throwing rocks and bottles and

Ohio National Guardsmen set up machine-gun posts on the street corners on May 24, 1934, during a strike at the Auto-Lite plant. *Toledo–Lucas County Public Library.*

taunting the guardsmen and the guardsmen firing tear gas canisters and charging into the crowd with fixed bayonets.

Around 3:00 p.m., after firing warning shots into the air, the National Guard fired into the crowd of protesters, killing twenty-seven-year-old Frank Hubay, who was shot four times, and twenty-year-old Stephen Cyigon and wounding a dozen others. Guardsmen's bullets wounded 2 more later that night, and 10 guardsmen were treated after being hit by bricks. Another 400 troops were called in as reinforcements.

There was a lull on Friday, May 25, but another full-scale battle erupted on Saturday, May 26, when five thousand protesters clashed with the National Guard. Two hundred demonstrators were wounded, and fifty protesters were arrested.

The violence became known as "the Battle of Chestnut Hill," ending when the National Guard withdrew on May 31. Auto-Lite management and Local 18384 signed an agreement on June 2 giving the union the right to bargain for plant workers. Workers received a 5 percent wage increase and a minimum wage of thirty-five cents an hour.

Strikers and supporters clashed with the National Guard near the Auto-Lite plant in what became known as the Battle of Chestnut Hill. *Toledo–Lucas County Public Library.*

Two people were killed when guardsmen opened fire at protesters during the 1934 Auto-Like strike, a turning point in U.S. labor history. *Toledo–Lucas County Public Library.*

The Auto-Lite factory reopened on June 5. The Federal Labor Union's success led to widespread unionization in Toledo and other auto factories, including Chevrolet in 1935.

Auto-Lite was acquired by Ford Motor Company in 1961, and the Detroit automaker began using Auto-Lite products as standard factory equipment in its vehicles.

BIRTH OF THE JEEP

It was the Willys-Overland Company that created the Jeep prototype based on U.S. military specifications for a lightweight, four-wheel-drive reconnaissance vehicle. The first working version of what became known as the Jeep was actually produced by American Bantam Car Co., a small carmaker founded in 1929 in Butler, Pennsylvania.

In June 1940, the U.S. Army's quartermaster corps invited 135 automakers to design a four-wheel-drive vehicle with a rectangular body, a maximum weight of 1,300 pounds, a wheelbase of eighty inches or less, a

Jeeps were tested for their durability, including being able to drive through high water. *Toledo–Lucas County Public Library.*

height of forty inches or less, ground clearance of six and a half inches and a monopod mount for a .30-caliber gun. It had to be able to carry at least three people and pull a trailer of at least five hundred pounds. The military's invitation came with a tight deadline: a prototype had to be produced within forty-nine days and seventy vehicles manufactured within seventy-five days.

Bantam enlisted the help of Karl K. Probst, one of the country's leading engineers, and was the only automaker to meet the deadline. The "Bantam Number One" prototype was delivered to the army's Camp Holabird in Baltimore at 4:30 p.m. on September 23, 1940—just half an hour before the deadline expired. The vehicle had a four-cylinder, forty-five horsepower engine, a three-speed transmission and a cost of $1,166 per unit.

Only two other automakers, Willys-Overland and Ford, responded to the military's invitation, but neither was able to meet the deadline for producing a prototype. While the Bantam model underwent three weeks of testing at Camp Holabird, Willys and Ford sent company engineers to observe the results.

Bantam officials protested the army's decision to let their competitors view the prototype, but the army's quartermaster responded that the prototype was now government property and he could allow whoever he wanted to examine the Bantam Number One.

A number of Jeep historians believe the real reason the army allowed Willys and Ford to monitor the tests was that the government was skeptical of Bantam's ability to mass produce the vehicles if an order were placed. The army wanted to protect its interests by letting the more established automakers be involved.

Willys delivered its prototype, the Quad, on November 11, 1940, and Ford turned over its prototype, dubbed the Pygmy, on November 23. The military then ordered 1,500 vehicles from each of the three manufacturers. The Willys cost $739 per vehicle, and the Ford cost $1,200.

Amending its initial specifications, the army raised the weight limit to 2,160 pounds, but the Willys prototype was still more than 200 pounds too heavy. Willys engineers pored over every part of the car, reducing the weight until the final prototype was so close to the limit that "even a little dust or mud could have taken the vehicle over the regulation limit," wrote Colonel C.C. Duel, the army liaison at Camp Holabird.

Sometime during the testing period, the vehicle became known as a Jeep. The precise origin of the name is not clear, but one theory is that it was derived from the military designation "GP," for General Purpose. But the prototypes were never intended for general purpose, so that theory seems

Jeeps were shipped all over the globe, including 630,000 manufactured during World War II. *Toledo–Lucas County Public Library.*

unlikely. Another, more probable, explanation is that "jeep" was military slang for any new and untested product. A Willys test driver, Red Hausman, was asked about the prototype vehicle by a reporter for the *Washington Daily News* and responded, "It's a jeep," according an article published on February 21, 1941. In an accompanying photo, the caption labeled the Willys Quad "a Jeep." Hausman said he intentionally used the word Jeep a lot at Holabird, seeking to distinguish the Willys model from the competition.

The Willys Quad featured a sixty-horsepower "Go Devil" engine, the most powerful of the three prototypes, and fared the best in the Camp Holabird tests. The Willys was also the cheapest to produce, a key consideration for some of the army's top brass. On July 23, 1941, the quartermaster corps signed a contract with Willys to produce sixteen thousand Jeeps.

In October 1941, the army anticipated such a huge demand for Jeeps that it signed an agreement with Willys letting a second supplier use its drawings to produce more vehicles. Ford signed a $14.6 million contract with the military in November 1941, to produce 15,000 Jeeps. Willys manufactured more

Jeeps made by the Willys-Overland Motor Co. await shipment at the Rossford Ordnance Depot. *Toledo–Lucas County Public Library.*

than 350,000 Jeeps during World War II, and Ford ended up manufacturing another 280,000 before the war ended.

Bantam, which played a pivotal role in the development of the Jeep, never received another order from the military for vehicles after the initial deal for 1,500. The company manufactured trailers and aeronautical gear for the rest of World War II and ended up going out of business in 1956.

With approximately 630,000 Jeeps manufactured and shipped around the world during the war, Willys and other automakers were concerned that returning them to the United States would hurt sales of their new vehicles. Government officials were worried that bringing the Jeeps back home would hurt the domestic economy. As a result, most wartime Jeeps were scrapped, sold overseas, given to Allies or dumped into the sea. A nationwide sale of 10,000 surplus Jeeps, priced at $782 and under, was met with limited interest.

Willys began making plans for postwar production of the Jeep as early as 1944, a year before the end of World War II. The wartime exploits of the Jeep had been written about in the media and publicized to the point that Jeep was a blue-chip brand. The *New York Times*, for example, lauded the Jeep in a July 1945 editorial:

> *The Jeep is no limousine for long hauls, but it will carry the farmer and his family to market and the movies or a hundred and one errands speedily and with reasonable comfort. It will also serve as a useful workhorse for many specialized applications as well, in field or barn yard. The unusual degree of traction developed by its four-wheel drive makes it one of the most interesting motor vehicles to appear in many years.*

Willys took advantage of the Jeep's hero status, shifting its image to appeal to the postwar car buyer. Advertisements began making reference to Jeeps in peacetime: "Tomorrow, make your first new postwar car a Willys—a Jeep in Civvies."

In 1945, Willys began producing its first civilian Jeep, the CJ-1, soon followed by the CJ-2, or the "Agri-Jeep," for its farm-based uses. The CJ-2A could be hooked to such farm implements as plows, harrows, pasture cultivators, six-foot mowers or terracing blades. Willys ads and promotional literature often compared Jeeps to farm tractors but better because they could not only plow fields but also serve as a year-round utility vehicle with "field comfort" with doors, backrests and heaters. As a 1946 Willys ad put it: "Farmers get more work hours and more year-'round usefulness from their one investment in the 'Jeep.' To pull plows and harrows; to power hammer-mills, ensilage cutters and silo fillers; or to bring supplies from town…this one vehicle does 'em all. That's why farmers say: 'Get A Jeep.'"

In addition to selling Jeeps for agricultural purposes, Willys was confident its four-wheel-drive vehicles would have a special appeal for hunters, fishermen, contractors, oil drillers and other civilians wanting rugged and versatile vehicles.

Willys-Overland continued to design modified versions of its battle-tested Jeep for the civilian market in the years immediately following World War II. It introduced the popular wood-paneled Jeep wagon in 1946 (with a base price of $1,337), a Jeep pickup truck with the option of two-wheel or four-wheel drive in 1947 and the convertible Jeepster in October 1947.

In 1949, labor strife at some Jeep suppliers disrupted production at the Toledo factory. In addition, with one-third of Jeep's sales going to the agricultural market, sales plummeted when U.S. farmers suffered a bad year in 1949. Production fell from 100,000 Jeeps and Jeep trucks in 1948 to 36,000 the next year (although station wagon sales held steady at 22,300). The company's net income dropped from $7.1 million in 1948 to $3.4 million in 1949.

The 1950 Korean War revived the Jeep business, as the U.S. government in June ordered 4,000 Jeeps in just a month and later signed another

King Michael I of Romania inspects a Toledo-made Jeepster in 1947. *Toledo–Lucas County Public Library.*

contract for 8,350 more. The two orders combined for $34.4 million in Jeep sales. The next year, the government signed another deal with Jeep worth $63 million.

As Jeep sales soared with the military orders, Willys-Overland drew the attention of industrialist Henry Kaiser, who had been involved in the construction of the Hoover Dam and whose shipyard produced hundreds of vessels during World War II.

Kaiser entered automotive manufacturing in 1943 with production of the "Henry J," America's first compact car. The automobile had front-wheel drive, an aluminum body and was priced at less than $1,000. Its engine was manufactured by Willys-Overland.

In February 1953, Ward Canaday, president of Willys-Overland, disclosed that Kaiser was seeking to merge the two auto making firms. A month later, on March 24, 1953, an announcement was made that Kaiser had purchased Willys-Overland for $62.3 million. The combined companies were renamed the Willys Corporation, and with combined assets of more than $200 million, it marked the largest merger in automotive history at the time.

The company was renamed the Kaiser-Jeep Corporation in 1963 to take advantage of the Kaiser name. When sales of company's flagship CJ-5 model began to fall, Kaiser-Jeep found itself in need of production dollars to expand its line. The automaker was purchased by American Motors Corporation in 1970, renamed AMC-Jeep and began focusing its sales efforts on young car buyers.

By the end of the 1970s, the U.S. auto industry was fighting for its survival against an influx of Japanese and European imports. The Mideast oil crisis sent gas prices skyrocketing, helping boost sales of the more fuel-efficient imports.

Jeep's ownership went through a series of changes as French automaker Renault gained a controlling interest in AMC-Jeep in 1980, and Chrysler Corporation bought AMC-Jeep in August 1987. Chrysler merged with DaimlerBenz in 1999, forming DaimlerChrysler, and Daimler sold off the Chrysler unit in 2007.

When Chrysler filed for Chapter 11 bankruptcy reorganization in 2009, Italian automaker Fiat became a principal owner along with the U.S. and Canadian governments. In 2014, Fiat acquired enough shares to become the majority owner of Chrysler, forming Fiat Chrysler Automobiles, the seventh-largest automaker in the world.

FCA has two main assembly plants in Toledo, which in 2014 was manufacturing the Jeep Cherokee and the Jeep Wrangler models. In 2015, city and state officials were in discussions with FCA to keep production of the Jeep Wrangler in Toledo. The Wrangler, the closest modern relative of the military Jeep, has been manufactured in Toledo since 1992, but FCA's leadership suggested in early 2015 that its Toledo facilities may not be suitable for the redesigned model due in 2017.

The original Toledo Jeep Parkway plant, which began as the American Bicycle Co. in 1902 and where the first Jeeps were manufactured in 1941, underwent demolition starting in 2002. In 2015, the only visible reminder of the factory is a towering brick smokestack emblazoned with the word "OVERLAND" in vertical lettering.

10

NEIGHBORHOODS

IDENTITY AND TRADITION

As Toledo's population soared from 1,222 in 1840 to 243,164 in 1920, much of the city's growth came from German, Polish, Hungarian and Irish immigrants arriving with big hopes and small resources. Many came to America seeking political and religious freedom or with dreams of financial advancement. A large number had no other choice; they were forced to flee persecution, famine or poverty in their homelands. When these new Toledo residents settled in with jobs, homes and newfound liberty, they wrote letters back home boasting of their adventures, writing stories that inspired their aunts and uncles, siblings and cousins to follow in their footsteps and pursue a new life in America.

Immigrants naturally gravitated to neighborhoods where their friends and relatives were living, creating ethnic enclaves where the new arrivals could speak their native language and keep their customs while beginning the process of assimilating into a new culture. Their ethnic heritage was reinforced by fellow immigrants who spoke the same language, working and living alongside them or serving them at neighborhood grocery stores, butcher shops, bakeries, shoe stores and other businesses that kept a touch of the Old Country alive in the New World.

LENK'S HILL

The earliest immigrant groups that settled in northwest Ohio in large numbers were the Germans. Although Germany was not a nation until 1871, the region of thirty-nine independent states shared a common language, which was the thread that brought them together in America.

A large number of German immigrants settled in the farmlands surrounding Toledo, finding jobs in the fields, doing the work they had done back home. Numerous rural towns and villages in Ohio with names such as Van Wert, New Bremen, Minster and Ottoville reflect the heritage of these early German settlers. Many of the farm workers who crossed the Atlantic had dreams of owning their own farms someday, something they would never have been able to do in their native land because of class structure and social constraints.

In the city of Toledo, a thriving German neighborhood flourished just southwest of downtown in an area known as Lenk's Hill. Eventually spanning fifty blocks centered at Nebraska Avenue and City Park Avenue, the German neighborhood grew largely from the efforts of Peter Lenk, who had immigrated to Toledo from Wurzburg, Bavaria, in 1848. Lenk was just eighteen years old when he left his home country to escape the oppressive reign of King Ludwig I. Born into a prominent family, Lenk had been given a brewery when he was seventeen years old, and when he settled in Toledo, he soon established a winery and, in 1856, founded the Toledo Brewing and Malt Company.

Lenk recruited many of the newly arriving Germans to work in his brewery and winery. An astute businessman, he bought land and built houses for the new Toledoans, laying the groundwork for the German neighborhood that would thrive from the 1870s until the 1950s. He left a large greenspace open for a neighborhood park, where the workers and their families could get away from their small houses and socialize with neighbors. In 1930, census figures showed sixteen thousand residents living in the Lenk's Hill neighborhood.

After finding or building their homes, the next thing most new Americans wanted to build was a church. For the Germans who settled in Toledo, that meant establishing either a Roman Catholic parish or a Lutheran church. Churches in many ways were the center of the community, not just a place to worship but also for their social lives and for education, with many churches starting their own schools.

The first German Catholic church in Toledo was St. Mary Parish on Cherry Street, established in 1854. The parish was founded by Germans who had been attending St. Francis de Sales Church, the city's first Catholic church and the diocese's original cathedral, on Cherry and Superior Streets. The growing number of German immigrants led St. Mary to hold separate Masses in German and to enlarge the church building. In November 1853, a group of two hundred Germans petitioned for permission to start a German-language parish. The Right Reverend Amadeus Rappe, St. Francis's former pastor who had been elevated to bishop of Cleveland (which oversaw Toledo before the Toledo diocese was established in 1910), appointed Father Charles Evrard as pastor of German Catholics in Toledo and the surrounding area.

St. Mary Catholic Church was located just three blocks west of St. Francis de Sales, on the southwest corner of Cherry and Michigan Streets. The property cost $5,000 and the building $12,000, which parishioners paid off within eight years. The first High Mass was held on Rosary Sunday 1856, with Bishop Rappe as celebrant, and the building was dedicated on March 25, 1857.

The church opened a school run by Ursuline sisters in its basement, and the pastor lived in a residence at the rear of the basement. Both St. Mary and St. Francis established cemeteries, side by side, just north of the city limits at Lagrange Street and Manhattan Boulevard. Both cemeteries were incorporated into the Toledo diocese's Mount Carmel Cemetery.

As Toledo's German Catholic population continued to increase, Bishop Rappe saw the need to create a second German parish, establishing Saints Peter and Paul Church on St. Clair Street in Lenk's Hill. Just two miles from St. Mary's, the newly built church opened in 1866 and started a school, but both facilities were outgrown by the waves of German arrivals. A bigger church was built and dedicated in December 1875.

More than a decade before immigrants established the city's first German-language Catholic parish, Protestants who arrived from Germany had already founded Salem Lutheran Church in Vistula, a village that merged with Port Lawrence in 1837 to form the city of Toledo. Salem was founded on January 17, 1842, and built its first sanctuary in 1844. The church's current brick Gothic building, with its steeple looming high over the surrounding neighborhood, was erected in 1871 for a total cost of $12,000. Salem's steady growth led to the start of several other historic Lutheran congregations in the region, including St. Paul's Lutheran downtown in 1857, First St. John's Lutheran in East Toledo in 1860, St. John's Church and Epiphany Lutheran Church in South Toledo and St. John's in Williston.

Today Salem is located in a struggling neighborhood on the edge of downtown Toledo, where the church serves more than forty thousand hot meals a year and provides many other forms of outreach to its urban neighbors, funded in large part by more prosperous suburban Lutheran congregations.

Of all the ethnic festivals in Toledo, the annual German-American Festival is the largest. Held every year at the end of August, the three-day festival promotes German and Swiss cultures with parades, music, skits, sports, pretzel-eating competitions and *steinstossen*—throwing a 138-pound stone (the record, set by Kevin Marx in 2009, is fifteen feet, three and a half inches).

LAGRINKA AND KUSCHWANZ

As Polish Catholics began arriving in Toledo after the U.S. Civil War, many attended the German-language services at St. Mary's Catholic Church. At the time, the nation of Poland had been erased from the map and divided among Russia, Austria and Prussia. Most Poles who came to Toledo during that era left regions that were controlled by the German Kingdom of Prussia (which in 1871

Two women make paczki, a popular Polish pastry similar to doughnuts, in Toledo's Lagrinka neighborhood, circa 1990. *Toledo–Lucas County Public Library.*

The 211-foot steeple of St. Anthony Catholic Church towers over the Polish Kuschwanz neighborhood in Toledo. *Author's collection.*

became part of the Empire of Germany). Many were fleeing the *kulturkampf*, or "culture-struggle," imposed by Prussian prime minister (later chancellor of Germany) Otto von Bismarck, who sought to unify the region by forcing its diverse citizenry to speak German and abandon their ethnic traditions.

Some of the German-speaking priests spoke Polish, but most Poles knew enough German to say confession and understand the liturgy. Some Polish priests from Chicago also made occasional pastoral visits to Toledo to hear confessions.

The Poles settled into two distinct communities in Toledo. One became known as *Lagrinka*, a North Toledo neighborhood that developed around the main business route of Lagrange Street. The other bordered the Lenk's Hill German enclave in South Toledo, moving into a rural area that became known as *Kuschwanz*, or "Cow's Tail."

Most of the homes in both neighborhoods were modest, wood-frame buildings set on narrow lots that were thirty or forty feet wide. The new arrivals took great pride in keeping their lawns immaculately maintained and their houses spotlessly clean. People were friendly and were quick to help one another out. Some new arrivals kept chickens, rabbits and even pigs in their backyards and grew vegetables that they stored in root cellars during the winter, reflecting their rural upbringing in Poland.

Poles who did not speak English or who lacked education often took the hardest, most labor-intensive jobs, working long and hard hours at railroads, factories and breweries. After work, with their small homes and large families, many of the men frequented the bars and pool halls to relax.

There were numerous musical groups, including the Woodsmen of the World, the Silver Comet Band, the Polka Knights, Crusade and the Polka Dots Orchestra, that played polkas and other traditional favorites at parties, dances and weddings that were often celebrated for several days. Musician Dave Banasiak recalled polka music permeating the Polish neighborhoods: "During the warm months when doors and windows were opened, you could hear polka music played from homes, bars and halls." He said his band, the Polka Knights, used to practice in his backyard, and the neighbors would dance to the music in their own yards.

The first Polish church in Toledo, St. Hedwig, was founded in 1875, with Bishop Richard Gilmour of Cleveland appointing the Reverend Vincent Lewandowski as pastor. The decision on where to locate the first Polish parish was a matter of intense debate, as the two growing Polish communities were about six miles apart. There was some discussion on building the new church midway between the two neighborhoods, near Collingwood Boulevard and Monroe Street, but ultimately it was decided to build it in the heart of Lagrinka.

Many Polish Catholics walked the six miles from their homes in Kuschwanz to Mass at St. Hedwig, although a large number of Poles continued to attend German-language services at nearby Saints Peter and Paul Church. Later, a trolley line was built that connected the two neighborhoods, leading some to call it the longest trolley line on earth since it went "from Pole to Pole."

The city's second Polish Catholic parish, St. Anthony Church on Nebraska Avenue, started as a mission to the Kuschwanz community by St. Hedwig's Parish and its founding pastor, Father Lewandowski. St. Anthony's became an independent parish in 1881, and ten years later, an imposing Gothic brick building with a 211-foot steeple was built. Its pews could seat 1,600, and the parish reached a peak membership of 8,000 in the 1950s.

The wave of Polish immigrants to Toledo continued into the early twentieth century, and a second Lagrinka parish, St. Adalbert, was established in 1908. The initial membership of St. Adalbert was 150 families, but in less than twenty years, church membership had grown to more than 1,000, leading to construction of a new and larger building dedicated by Bishop Samuel Stritch on

April 28, 1928. Three other Catholic churches were established in Kuschwanz: St. Stanislaus Kostka (1908), Nativity (1922) and St. Hyacinth (1927).

All of Toledo's Polish Catholic parishes thrived for decades but began losing members in the 1950s and '60s, an era when Toledoans began moving from the city to the suburbs. Nativity, for example, had 1,920 members in 1952, but only 185 when it was closed in 1980. St. Anthony had just 400 members and St. Stanislaus 300 when Toledo Bishop Leonard Blair closed the parishes in 2005. St. Hyacinth continues to serve the few Poles still living in Kuschwanz, and Lagrinka's two Polish Catholic parishes were merged in 2010 to form the Parish of St. Adalbert and St. Hedwig.

After the Polish parishes were closed in 2005 as part of an overall realignment of the Toledo diocese, several Catholics who were dissatisfied at losing their home parishes joined together and started the Resurrection Polish National Catholic Church, a denomination that is Catholic but not Roman Catholic. They met at several different locations before buying a former Protestant church just north of Toledo in Temperance, Michigan, in 2008. Resurrection PNCC parishioners continue to honor their Polish heritage, although Mass is said in English.

The former rectory of St. Anthony Church in Kuschwanz has been turned into a neighborhood outreach center with classes for children on everything from gardening to drumming. Sister Virginia Welsh started the ministry, called the Padua Center, and in 2010 held a "Name the Neighborhood" contest, pointing out that Kuschwanz no longer fit because there were few Poles still living there. The winning entry was "Kwanzaa Park," although the new name has yet to gain acceptance.

Toledo still flies its Polish colors every year when the Lagrange Street Polish Festival is held in July. Tens of thousands turn out for two days and nights of polka music, traditional dance by troupes such as Echoes of Poland, pierogi-eating contests and various other Polish-themed entertainment and food, with guests consuming forty thousand pierogi and three hundred kegs of beer over the festival weekend.

ARRIVAL OF THE IRISH

Another significant wave of Toledo immigrants came from Ireland, where periods of economic strife, political oppression and famine spurred millions to cross the Atlantic either to survive or in search of better lives. The earliest record of an Irish immigrant in northwest Ohio dates to 1796, when Father Edmund Burke served as a missionary to Native Americans near Fort Miami, the present-day site of the suburb of Maumee.

Late blight, a disease caused by a wind-blown fungus, destroyed 40 percent of Ireland's potato crop in 1845 and virtually the entire crop in 1846, causing mass starvation among Irish peasants. Potatoes had been their primary source of food for half a century, mixed with milk to provide almost all of their nutrition. They also grew wheat, oats and barley, but the landlords took those crops as rent. An estimated 1 million people starved as a result of the famine, and up to 2 million of Ireland's population of 8.4 million left the country between 1844 and 1851.

Many of the Irish immigrants to America first settled on the East Coast and then migrated west as they worked on railroads and canals. The digging of the Miami and Erie Canal and the Wabash Canal and the building of the Erie and Kalamazoo Railroad brought the first wave of Irish workers to Toledo in the 1830s. After construction of the railroads was completed, many Irishmen found good jobs working for the railroad companies. By 1850, 620 of Toledo's population of 3,829 had been born in Ireland. Irish neighborhoods developed on the southern edge of downtown Toledo and in East Toledo. The 1870 census reported 3,032 Irish-born residents, nearly 10 percent of the city's population of 31,584.

Most of the Irish newcomers were Roman Catholic, and parishes that were established to serve their communities became linchpins of the Irish-American neighborhoods. St. Patrick's Church, now known as St. Patrick's Historic, was founded in 1863 and Immaculate Conception Church, known as "Old Darby," in 1868, both south of the city. Good Shepherd Church was established in East Toledo in 1873.

The first St. Patrick's Church, under the leadership of Irish-born priest Father Edward Hannin, opened on February 2, 1867, at Lafayette and Thirteenth Streets. The brick church was built for $27,000 plus donated labor and materials. Father Hannin also opened St. Patrick's Academy, a school that had four hundred students taught by four Ursuline nuns and four lay teachers. Construction began on a second, much larger St. Patrick's Church in 1892, but because of an economic downturn, the building was not completed until 1901.

Meanwhile, the Irish immigrants opened businesses and built homes in the area surrounding the church. Among the Irish-owned businesses were blacksmith shops, grocery stores, butcher shops, lumberyards, funeral homes and saloons.

Immaculate Conception was built across Swan Creek in what is now called the Old South End, serving the new wave of Irish immigrants from counties Mayo and Kerry. The Old South End was a transportation hub, with several railroad lines converging in the neighborhood, providing jobs for many of the Irish arrivals. The church was built at Western and Sumner Streets in 1870, and its debt was paid off in 1888. The present Immaculate Conception Church, on Western Avenue, was dedicated on November 16, 1896.

Good Shepherd was established after sixty families petitioned for an Irish parish in East Toledo in 1872. Parishioners started out meeting in a building owned by the Pennsylvania Railroad at Oakdale and Miami Streets before building a combination of church and school on Clark Street in 1873. The building was surrounded by cornfields when it first opened, but as the neighborhood developed over the next few decades, the parish flourished. By 1902, Good Shepherd was the home parish of three hundred families and two thousand members.

Toledo's Irish neighborhoods thrived until after World War II, when city dwellers moved to the suburbs. The shifting demographics were magnified by several factors that hastened the end of Toledo's Irish neighborhoods. For one, the decline of the local railroad industry meant fewer jobs for the

Mario Terero's mural of Martin Luther King Jr. covers a wall in Toledo's Old South End, a former Irish neighborhood that is now mostly Hispanic. *Author's collection.*

Irish residents of the Old South End and East Toledo. Another contributing factor was the building of Interstate 75 in the 1950s, which cut through the middle of the St. Patrick's Historic's parish boundaries, isolating the church from many of its members.

By 1970, Irish neighborhoods had virtually disappeared from Toledo. By 2015, the Old South End had become the center of Toledo's Hispanic community.

BIRMINGHAM AND IRONVILLE

Across the Maumee River in East Toledo, Hungarians began moving into East Toledo's Birmingham neighborhood after it made the transition from agriculture to industry in the late 1800s. The National Malleable Castings Company, based in Cleveland, gave the neighborhood's Hungarian heritage a jump-start in 1890, when it transferred two hundred Hungarian workers to the foundry's new plant on Front Street in Toledo. Most of the Hungarian workers had emigrated from north-central Hungary counties such as Abuja, Gomer and Heves.

"To us, they were just as foreign as if they came from the moon," said Edna Nofziger, who had grown up in Birmingham. "They were really aliens. They dressed differently, of course. The women wore babushkas…and they went barefooted."

The new arrivals planted vegetable gardens and kept chickens, geese and, after saving enough money, cows to feed their families, Nofziger told an interviewer. "Every bit of land that could be cultivated was cultivated. They were very industrious and tried to be very good providers for their families."

The men worked long hours and were paid seven or eight dollars a week. Some families supplemented their income by keeping boarders, opening spare bedrooms to the single men who had arrived from Hungary to work at the foundry. Birmingham residents said crime was not a concern around the turn of the twentieth century, and people kept their front doors unlocked. Priests and ministers used to walk the neighborhood, keeping an eye on the youth and making sure they didn't get into trouble.

More factories, foundries and industry came to East Toledo over the next several decades, including the United States Malleable, Maumee Malleable Castings, Toledo Edison (then known as Rail Light Company), two coal yards and a cement-block manufacturer. With the new industry and job

Two landmarks of Toledo's Birmingham neighborhood: Tony Packo's Café and the Church of St. Stephen, King of Hungary. *Author's collection*

opportunities, East Toledo's population more than doubled from eighteen thousand in 1900 to forty thousand in 1920, including five thousand Hungarians. The Hungarians, along with smaller numbers of emigrants from other Slavic and Central European nations, lived in modest "worker cottages"—one-story buildings with no indoor plumbing.

Most of the Hungarian immigrants were Roman Catholics who lived within the boundaries of Sacred Heart Parish but were visited by a Hungarian Catholic priest from Cleveland. In 1898, the first Hungarian ethnic parish in Birmingham was founded by one hundred families: the Church of St. Stephen, King of Hungary.

The church, as in Toledo's other ethnic neighborhoods, was a center of community life not only for births, weddings and funerals but also in carrying on folk customs from their native land. One such tradition was "Dousing Day," observed on the Monday after Easter, when young men would throw water on young women or dump them in a horse-watering trough. In Birmingham, the Dousing Day rituals were refined, and the young men asked permission to sprinkle the young lady, sometimes with perfume. The next day, Tuesday after Easter, it was the young girls' turn to douse the boys.

The Hungarian Christmas play *Bethlemes Jatek* is performed at St. Stephen's Catholic Church. *Toledo–Lucas County Public Library.*

Another church tradition brought back from the Old Country was the centuries-old Christmas Nativity play *Bethlehemes Jatek*. The play involves shepherds, angels and "oregs," or mean-looking old men, and was performed for decades every Christmas Eve at St. Stephen Church. But by the late 1990s, so few Birmingham residents spoke Hungarian that the play was discontinued. It was revived for a few years from 2001 to 2007, but the actors had to learn their Hungarian-language parts phonetically because they didn't speak the language. The play has not been performed for almost a decade.

A small group of Protestants that emigrated from Hungary founded the Magyar Reformatus Egyhaz, or Hungarian Reformed Church, on June 16, 1903, which in 1962 became Calvin United Church of Christ. The church still holds services in Hungarian and continues such traditions as baking bread and making noodles using Old World recipes.

The Birmingham community's Hungarian heritage was threatened during the First and Second World Wars, when Hungary fought against the United States and immigrants were encouraged to become more "Americanized." But Hungarian pride resurged in 1956 with Hungary's rebellion against Soviet occupation. When the Soviet Union quashed the rebellion, thousands of Hungarian freedom fighters fled to the United States. The first refugee families arrived on November 27, 1956, and a total of about three hundred more settled in Toledo. One-fourth of the "56ers" moved into the Birmingham neighborhood, giving the community a renewed sense of ethnic pride.

One of the enduring landmarks of Birmingham's Hungarian heritage is Tony Packo's, the East Toledo restaurant famous for its Hungarian hot dog. The restaurant was started by Tony Packo, born in 1908 to Hungarian immigrants, who had worked in a factory until borrowing $100 from relatives to start a sandwich and ice cream shop in 1932. Three years later, Tony and his wife, Rose, had earned enough money to buy the wedge-shaped building at Front and Consaul Streets, near St. Stephen's Church, where the main restaurant is still located.

Packo's became a global brand in 1976, when Jamie Farr, the Toledo-born actor who played Korean War soldier Max Klinger, reminisced about his hometown in an episode of *M*A*S*H* and longed for a Packo's Hungarian hot dog. The Birmingham restaurant and its spicy hot dogs were mentioned in five more *M*A*S*H* scripts, and a gastronomic star was born. The restaurant's walls are decorated with hundreds of hot dog buns signed by celebrities—a tradition that started with Burt Reynolds in 1972.

Just north of Birmingham was another notable East Toledo neighborhood called Ironville. The neighborhood sprouted in the 1860s, when a pig-iron smelting business was built on a marshy plot that had once been home to Ottawa Indians. The neighborhood bounded by Front, Bay and Tiffin Streets and Clarence Avenue was known for the smoke and acrid smell spewed from the furnaces and refineries. Ironville residents were known for their thirst, as the neighborhood had five bars and only two grocery stores and two churches.

The demise of Ironville began in 1960, when the City of Toledo started buying houses to build an industrial park. Although 250 homes were purchased, the industrial park was never built. "All they've got there now is a junkyard," said Floyd Tefft.

Residents of the defunct community still gather annually for an Ironville reunion, talking about the good old days and sharing photos and memories. "Ironville was always a great place," Tefft said.

"It was a bit of a slum, and it smelled, but it wasn't as bad as they said," said Dr. Joe Hardin, a veterinarian.

North Toledo Amusements

On grassy strip of land in North Toledo where the Maumee River opens into Maumee Bay, seniors putt for par at the Bay View Retirees Golf Course, people stroll or walk their dogs at Bay View Park and a nearby wastewater plant converts raw sewage into methane fuel. It's a fairly quiet stretch of land today, but a century ago, it was a place that drew thrill seekers for roller coaster rides, casino gambling and watching professional baseball games.

Toledo's professional baseball team, then known as the Swamp Angels, played its weekend home games from 1896 to 1900 at Bay View Park, just north of the city line, to avoid Toledo's blue laws that prohibited baseball on Sundays. It was during the team's first year at Bay View, where scores of duck-like American coots congregated in the marshy fields, that the team's name was switched to the distinctive, enduring and beloved Mud Hens moniker.

The Lake Erie Casino opened in 1895, at the end of the electric streetcar line in Toledo's Point Place neighborhood. A boardwalk led the way to the three-story casino, which had slot machines, gambling tables, a 3,500-seat theater and Kinetescopes that showed a famous boxing match.

A switchback roller coaster took riders out over the water and then raced back to land, and the park offered other amusements such as a carousel, a crystal maze, a fun house with mirrors, fishponds, hot air balloons, a beer hall and fireworks. Frank Burt ran a playhouse featuring vaudeville and light opera.

Dr. Louis R. Effler, in his book *My Memoirs of the Gay 90's*, recalled the thrills of going to the casino: "On Sundays…in addition to the performance—and the cooling breezes—and ice-cream sodas—there would be tub races and various other amusements! Oh, those were the days! The casino was 'the' place for many years."

The wooden buildings, coaster and boardwalk were vulnerable to fire, however, and a series of spectacular blazes ultimately brought about the casino's demise. The original building burned down in 1899, and the owners opened a new casino on the same spot the following year. The new casino was built on pilings above the water at the end of a one-thousand-foot boardwalk. In December 1901, another fire struck the casino, and a third incarnation opened on June 1, 1902, with a boardwalk that was extended several hundred feet and decorated with a canopy of five thousand red, white and blue incandescent bulbs.

When an intense blaze struck the casino just before the Fourth of July celebration in 1910, the entire structure was destroyed in less than forty-five minutes. This time the owners chose not to rebuild.

On June 21, 1929, another amusement park opened in Point Place, just north of the former casino site, called Willow Beach Park. The park, built at a cost of half a million dollars, offered everything from kiddie rides and entertainment for the children to dining, dancing and gambling for the adults. Admission was only twenty-five cents and included parking—in a lot that could accommodate three thousand cars.

An advertisement promoting Willow Beach's grand opening called it "Toledo's Playground" and "the last word in amusement and recreation." It advertised "ideal bathing beaches, fine dance pavilion, every popular new ride, picnic groves." Rides included "Bobs Coaster," a whirling "Bug Ride," a "Kiddies' Auto Ride" and a seaplane.

The park opened just before the Great Depression and suffered another setback in 1932, when it was damaged by a fire. Willow Beach closed in 1949, and in 1954, the City of Toledo bought the property for $50,000 and installed a boat ramp and marina.

OLD WEST END

When Toledo became a city in 1837, most residents lived downtown or in the immediate vicinity. As the central business district expanded farther west of the Maumee River, some of Toledo's wealthiest families also moved westward, building in a new subdivision that became known as the Old West End. The neighborhood was platted in 1870 by Frank J. Scott, son of Toledo pioneer Jesup W. Scott, on family land and was less than two miles from downtown. Yet the area was still considered "the woods."

The land, inhabited for generations by Ottawa Indians, was first sold by the U.S. government in 1817 for $1.25 an acre. Early settlers included Major Coleman I. Keeler, who in 1818 built a log cabin near the present site of Rosary Cathedral, and Noah A. Whitney Sr., who in 1824 settled eighty acres of land with his wife, five sons and five daughters.

From 1870 until 1920, the Old West End was Toledo's most prestigious neighborhood. The area bounded by Monroe Street, Collingwood Boulevard, Central Avenue and Glenwood Avenue featured large, ornate and elegant homes designed by the city's finest architects for Toledo's most prominent families. Many of the structures featured Old World craftsmanship, from Corinthian-capped columns and terrazzo floors to stone fireplaces and wood cabinetry. Streets were paved with specially treated cedar and pine blocks,

Collingwood Boulevard, in the heart of Toledo's Old West End, was known for its lush canopy of elm trees. *Toledo–Lucas County Public Library.*

reportedly to soften the sound of horses' hooves. The last of the wooden pavers disappeared in 1950 with the resurfacing of Robinwood Avenue.

Each of the Old West End homes was personalized for its owner, creating a colorful hodgepodge of architectural designs. Styles included Colonial Revival, Georgian Revival, Dutch Colonial, English Tudor, Queen Anne, Italian Renaissance, Victorian and Chateauesque. Prominent residents included Edward Ford, the president of the Edward Ford Glass Plate Company; Mayor Samuel "Golden Rule" Jones; Julius Lamson, owner of Lamson's department store; and Edward Drummond Libbey, Toledo glass pioneer.

One of the keystone houses in the Old West End was built by licorice tycoon Alvin B. Tillinghast on the corner of Robinwood Avenue and Bancroft Street in 1901. The original plans called for an additional wing along Bancroft, but it was never completed because Tillinghast went bankrupt during construction of the 8,300-square-foot English Tudor mansion. He turned the building over to the construction company, which in turn traded the brick-and-wood mansion to John Willys North, president of Willys-Overland Company, for twelve Pope-Toledo automobiles. The home has nine bedrooms, five and a half bathrooms and a foyer featuring a gold-

The 8,300-square-foot Tillinghast mansion on Robinwood Avenue, built in 1901, has nine bedrooms and five and a half bathrooms. *Toledo–Lucas County Public Library.*

leaf ceiling and a large stained-glass window. The mansion was for sale in early 2015, priced at $299,000.

Collingwood Boulevard was long known for a lush canopy of elm trees, so dense that one could walk down the street during a spring shower without feeling a drop of rain. Dutch elm disease decimated the elms in the 1960s, and seventy-two honey locusts planted to replace them were removed by the city in 2013 in order to access and replace aging water mains.

While there are several theories for the origin of the popular phrase "Holy Toledo," one widely held belief credits the phrase to the many magnificent churches and synagogues that lined both sides of Collingwood Boulevard. The imposing buildings included Collingwood Presbyterian Church; First Unitarian Church; Second Church of Christ, Scientist; First Congregational Church; Congregation Shomer Emunim; B'nai Jacob Synagogue; St. Mark's Episcopal Church; First Baptist Church; and the Toledo diocese's cathedral Mary, Queen of the Most Holy Rosary Cathedral (commonly known as Rosary Cathedral). The majestic cathedral is designed in a Spanish Plateresque architectural style with an exterior of Massachusetts granite and Indiana limestone. The cornerstone was laid

Right: Construction of Rosary Cathedral, the Toledo Catholic Diocese's cathedral, started in 1925 and was completed in 1940. *Author's collection.*

Opposite, bottom: This ten-thousand-square-foot mansion, designed by Edward O. Fallis for Charles Reynolds in 1887, was converted into an inn, which closed in 2015. *Toledo–Lucas County Public Library.*

in 1925, the first public service was held in 1931 and the cathedral was dedicated in October 1940.

Many of the Old West End's original congregations have moved out of the neighborhood, decisions that became necessary due to declining memberships and the prohibitive costs of the utilities and upkeep.

By the 1930s, the Old West End was no longer the city's most prestigious neighborhood. Residents were being lured to such new areas as Ottawa Hills and Old Orchard. The Old West End Association was formed in 1941 with a mission of preserving the historic neighborhood. The group succeeded in preventing an interstate highway from being built through the neighborhood in the 1960s and has worked to resolve issues that affect many urban neighborhoods, including white flight, crime and lack of good schools.

Today, the Old West End's twenty-five blocks contain one of the largest collections of late Victorian houses in the nation. The Old West End Festival, held every summer, draws tens of thousands to the historic neighborhood with a parade, concerts and arts and crafts shows.

First Congregational Church on Collingwood Boulevard moved into the Old West End in 1916. The church features eight Tiffany stained-glass windows. *Author's collection.*

11
ST. CLAIR STREET

TOLEDO'S "MINI TIMES SQUARE"

The Valentine Theatre, designed in a Sullivanesque style by Toledo architect Edward O. Fallis, opened on Christmas Day 1895 with an 8:00 p.m. performance by Joseph Jefferson III of his signature show, *Rip Van Winkle*.

When the curtain went up, the sixty-six-year-old actor greeted the sold-out crowd and commented that the Valentine was on par with some of the world's finest opera houses and theaters in which he had performed. The 1,900-seat theater at St. Clair and Adams Streets had been commissioned by banker George Ketcham, who also owned the Mud Hens and champion trotting horse Cresceus and was named after his late father, Valentine (who a few years earlier had become Toledo's first millionaire).

The theater boasted electric illumination, elegantly furnished boxes, Italian Renaissance–style sculptures, a white-and-ecru color scheme, twenty exits and a heating and cooling system that could produce an even temperature year-round.

Crowds of people eager to see the new theater gathered on the sidewalk a few hours before showtime and were held in check by police. The doors opened shortly after seven, and patrons "invariably stopped at the door and gave exclamations of delight at the entrancing scene before them," according to the next day's edition of the *Toledo Blade*. "The Valentine is in itself a standard of perfection, after which future play houses will be measured. It is the most complete and beautiful theatre west of the Alleghenies and has but few equals in the country."

The Valentine Theatre, shown here in 1937, opened in 1895, closed in 1972 and reopened in 1999 after a $28 million renovation. *Toledo–Lucas County Public Library.*

The stage was not the only attraction at the Valentine. On December 18, 1913, a crowd estimated at eight thousand gathered on St. Clair Street to see the unveiling of an electrical billboard atop the building, lit by seven thousand ten-watt bulbs, which proclaimed, "You will do better in Toledo." The slogan had been submitted by C.W. Lammers and selected from seven thousand entries in a contest sponsored by the Toledo Commerce Club. Measuring one hundred feet in width and fifty-eight feet in height, the sign was donated by the Toledo Railways and Light Commission. The sign remained in place until the 1960s, and in 2013, the slogan was revived, given a boost by Mayor D. Michael Collins, and has since become a popular local T-shirt.

The Valentine Theatre's heyday for live performances faded as "moving pictures" became popular, and projection facilities were added at the venue in 1914. The theater was renovated in 1942 and converted into a Loew's movie house.

The Valentine Theatre closed in 1972, and in 1983, a city task force recommended that the building be demolished. That suggestion sparked a community effort to save the theater and, sixteen years and $28 million later,

The St. Clair Street entrance of the Valentine Theatre, originally the venue's main doors, became the rear entrance after the 1999 renovation. *Author's collection.*

the Valentine Theatre was reborn. Completely revamped with a 901-seat auditorium, plush carpeting, velvet drapes and chandeliers, the Valentine continues to bring live theater, opera, ballet, Broadway shows and movies to Toledo audiences. An estimated 900,000 people have attended events at the theater since its 1999 reopening.

From the night of the Valentine's grand opening through 1920, thousands of performers, including many of the most famous names in show business, graced the venue's stage. The theater's board of directors in 1999 commissioned Toledo artist Paul Geiger to paint a mural featuring some of the stars who had performed at the theater. The resulting sixty-eight- by ten-foot mural, unveiled at the theater in 2008, includes such famous performers as W.C. Fields, Will Rogers, Fanny Brice, Harry Houdini, Bill "Mr. Bojangles" Robinson, Lionel Barrymore, Sarah Bernhardt, Anna Pavlova, Ed Wynn, Douglas Fairbanks Sr., "March King" John Philip Sousa, actress Lillian Russell, Vaslav Nijinsky and Al Jolson (plus a side-view cameo of the artist in a jester's cap).

The Valentine Theatre's renovation makes for a happy ending, unlike the scores of theaters that once thrived in downtown Toledo. Such popular entertainment venues as the Rivoli, the Palace, the Pantheon, the Granada and the Princess once lit up St. Clair Street like a miniature Times Square, with marquees displaying the names of the latest Hollywood movies and their stars. The theaters, clubs and bars gave Toledo a bit of big-city glamour and energy. Within several blocks were the Esquire Theater, the Loop and the Royal on Superior Street, the Gayety Burlesque on Summit Street and Burt's Theater and the Pythian Castle on Jefferson Avenue.

St. Clair Street became the center of Toledo's theater district starting in 1871, when the 1,400-seat Wheeler Opera House opened at the northwest corner of St. Clair and Monroe Streets. "It became known all over the theatrical world for its modern arrangements, its magnificent decorations, and its stage and lighting facilities," the *Pageant Press* reported.

The Wheeler's stage was seventy-seven feet wide, with a drop curtain of crimson and green damask. There were tilting, leather-upholstered seats near the front of the stage; frescoes in an arch over the stage portraying Shakespeare, Beethoven and Goethe; and a mammoth crystal chandelier hanging from the ceiling. When the playhouse opened on December 15, 1871, with Parepa Rosa's English Opera Company in *Bohemian Girl* and *Martha*, ticket-buyers waited in line at the box office up to four hours.

The stars who performed at the Wheeler included Sarah Bernhardt, Maurice Barrymore, Joseph Jefferson III and Buffalo Bill. In 1876, Toledo's first "legal" wrestling match was held at the theater, with Colonel McLaughlin of Detroit pitted against "Mr. Smith" of New York.

The Wheeler's owners took extra precautions for safety, especially fire, installing an iron tank on the roof that held 350 barrels of water and adding safety screens to keep the stage's canvas backdrops from coming in contact with burner lights. Despite their best efforts, the Wheeler Opera House burned to the ground on March 17, 1893. (Shortly after the fire, a commercial building known as the Wheeler Block was built on the site, which was demolished in the early 1980s.)

Another pioneering downtown theater was the 1,800-seat New People's Theater, which opened in 1885 at St. Clair and Orange Streets, presenting mostly B-level vaudeville and family shows. It was sold in 1899 and renamed the Lyceum Theater.

The Empire Theater, which opened at 424 St. Clair Street in 1901, started with vaudeville but by 1904 had switched to staging burlesque shows. It was renamed the Palace in 1919, showing movies until it was razed during Toledo's urban renewal efforts in 1969.

Theaters lined St. Clair Street downtown in 1935, making the street look like Toledo's version of Times Square. *Toledo–Lucas County Public Library.*

Keith's Theater opened in 1911 at 313 St. Clair Street. Designed by George Mills for vaudeville entrepreneur B.F. Keith, the theater brought in such stars as Sophie Tucker, Will Rogers and Harry Houdini. When movies started to become more of a draw than live shows, the Keith became a movie theater and was renamed the Cameo in 1930 and then the Grenada in 1932. It was demolished in 1957 for a parking lot.

The Princess, the Palace and the Rivoli were virtually all in a row on the east side of St. Clair Street, and the Granada, Pantheon and Loew's Valentine were across the street on the west side. The Rivoli, which opened in November 1920, and the Palace theaters both closed down on November 2, 1968. The Esquire, which opened in 1941 on North Superior Street, was the last remaining movie house in downtown Toledo before it went out of business in 1978. In the early1990s, the Esquire was renovated and turned into a concert venue, but the theater was demolished in 2007 to clear space for Huntington Arena.

St. Clair Street today is home to tall office buildings and parking garages, with only the rear entrance of the Valentine Theater remaining as a reminder of the glory days when the downtown street was Toledo's entertainment capital.

Burt's Theater opened on Jefferson Avenue at Ontario Street in September 1898 as a 1,500-seat opera house managed by Frank Burt. Designed by architect George Mills, the three-story building's strikingly ornate exterior was based on a fifteenth-century Venetian

The Pythian Castle on Jefferson Avenue, built in 1890, was turned into an artists' community in the 1970s but has been vacant for four decades. *Author's collection.*

palace, Ca Da Ono, with arched windows and Gothic-style balconies, patterned brickwork and gargoyles. Burt's presented opera, vaudeville and melodramas before being sold in 1908, after which it reopened as the American Music Hall, which presented live shows until 1916. The historic theater was revived as the Peppermint Club in the 1960s and in the 1990s became a bar known for female-impersonator stage shows. The building has been vacant since 2010, and a photo of the John Lennon mosaic in Central Park is displayed in one of its windows, offering one provocative word: "Imagine."

The Pythian Castle, at 801 Jefferson Avenue directly across Ontario Street from Burt's, is a dramatic, castle-like five-story structure topped by a 185-foot-tall turret. It was built for $38,000 in 1890, designed by Bacon and Huber to be the headquarters for the Knights of Pythias fraternal organization. In addition to meeting rooms and offices, the German Romanesque–style building also had recital rooms and two auditoriums for the J.W. Green Company, retail and wholesale dealer in pianos and organs. The Bleckner Music Company bought the building in 1960 and used it for music lessons and recitals.

In 1972, Toledo urban sociologist Edward Emery bought the Pythian Castle for $46,000, with dreams of turning the stone-and-brick castle into a center for the Toledo arts and music community. Rock concerts were held on weekends in the third-floor auditorium, with free movies shown during intermissions. Plans were made to open a Castle Crepes restaurant, a record store and a candle shop. "What we hope to do is give this dirty old building new life," Emery said. "You can't just bulldoze everything that's old."

Emery's arts community center did not last long, and the building has not had tenants since the mid-1970s. The castle was acquired by the Lucas County Land Bank in 2013, a government agency that seeks to prevent blight and make good use of vacant properties.

TOLEDO'S GRANDEST THEATER

The Paramount Theater, on the corner of Adams and Huron Streets, was the largest and most elegant movie theater ever built in Toledo. Designed in French Renaissance style by the Chicago architectural firm Rapp and Rapp, the Paramount opened on February 16, 1929, with a showing of *Redskin*, starring Richard Dix.

The Paramount Theater, which cost $3 million to build and opened in 1939 on the corner of Huron and Adams Streets, could seat 3,400 patrons. *Toledo–Lucas County Public Library.*

The $3 million theater could seat more than 3,400 patrons—1,589 in the orchestra, 394 in the mezzanine and 1,426 in the balcony. It had plush carpeting and terrazzo floors, gilded plaster relief, chandeliers and silk and brocade tapestries. An army of ushers wore military-like uniforms complete with brass buttons and highly polished shoes. Admission was twenty-five cents, more than double the ticket price of ten cents at competing theaters. Some Toledoans remember their families not being able to afford to the Paramount, walking right by the glorious theater to watch movies at nearby venues.

The Paramount's "atmospheric" auditorium included a painted canvas ceiling that mimicked the sky, with slowly drifting clouds or twinkling stars. Cool underground water was pumped from beneath the basement through the theater's plumbing system as a means of air-conditioning the building. The Paramount boasted one of Wurlitzer's finest pipe organs, which cost $55,000. It rose from the pit at the right of the stage, with the audience hearing the pipes come to life before seeing the organist. A stage band entertained audiences for fifteen minutes before the start of each movie.

The Paramount Theater's marquee lit up the night for movies, including this 1931 feature, *The Smiling Lieutenant*. *Toledo–Lucas County Public Library.*

Lasalle & Koch, the department store next to the Paramount, bought an ad in the *Toledo News-Bee* welcoming the Paramount to the neighborhood. It thanked the Publix Theatres Corporation for seeing fit "to make Toledo the home of the most modern theatre in the world, and the first to be built deliberately for sound and talking pictures. It is not too much to say that the opening today of the new Paramount Theatre is one of the most significant Toledo happenings in a decade." Patrons said the Paramount was so large and beautiful that it made them feel like they were going to a movie in the Taj Mahal.

In addition to showing first-run movies, the Paramount hosted famous entertainers on its stage, including a visit by Bob Hope and Roy Rogers in November 1942 to raise money for the War Chest. (Hope's and Rogers's appearances at seventeen theaters nationwide generated $1 million for U.S. war efforts.)

The theater never became profitable, however, burdened by its large initial debt and ongoing maintenance expenses. The popularity of television,

The Paramount Theater fell victim to the wrecking ball in 1965, and the property was turned into a parking lot. *Toledo–Lucas County Public Library.*

starting in the 1950s, also affected Americans' spending habits, taking customers away from the movie houses. The Paramount was demolished in 1965, and the site has been used as a parking lot ever since.

SELECTED BIBLIOGRAPHY

Abu-Absi, Samir, ed. *Arab Americans in Toledo: Cultural Assimilation and Community Involvement.* Toledo, OH: University of Toledo Press, 2010.

Ahern, John. *Birmingham Remembers: Transcriptions of Video-Taped Interviews 1983–1984.* University of Toledo Urban Affairs Center and the Toledo–Lucas County Library, 1986.

Barden, Thomas E., and John Ahern, eds. *Hungarian American Toledo: Life and Times in Toledo's Birmingham Neighborhood.* University of Toledo Urban Affairs Center, 2002.

Barden, Timothy, ed. *American Originals: Northwest Ohio's Polish Community at Work, Worship and Play.* Toledo, OH: University of Toledo Press, 2014.

Bourne, Russell. *Floating West: The Erie & Other American Canals.* New York: W.W. Norton, 1992.

Clark, Bob, Mike Childers, Tom Shaw and Larry Michaels. *The Streets of Toledo: A Pictorial History: 1920s–1970s.* Toledo, OH: Bihl House, 2008.

Downes, Randolph C. *Industrial Beginnings: Lucas County Historical Series.* Vol. 4. Toledo: Historical Society of Northwestern Ohio, 1954.

Floyd, Barbara L. *Toledo: The 20th Century.* Charleston, SC: Arcadia Publishing, 2005.

Hebert, Lou. *Day by Day in Toledo: An Almanac of the Interesting, Important, and Unusual Stories of Toledo's Past.* Toledo, OH: Herbert Media, 2013.

Husman, John R. *Baseball in Toledo: Images of Baseball.* Charleston, SC: Arcadia Publishing, 2003.

Kavieff, Paul R. *The Purple Gang: Organized Crime in Detroit 1910–1945*. Fort Lee, NJ: Barricade Books, 2000.

Kopytek, Bruce Allen. *Toledo's Three Ls: Lamson's, the Lion Store and Lasalle's*. Charleston, SC: The History Press, 2013.

Korth, Philip A., and Margaret R. Beegle. *I Remember Like Today: The Auto-Lite Strike of 1934*. East Lansing: Michigan State University Press, 1988.

Law and Labor: A Monthly Periodical on the Law of the Labor Problem. Vols. 3–4, October 1921. N.p.: League for Industrial Rights.

Mauk, Clint. *Historical Tales of Toledo*. Maumee, OH: Woodlands, 2004.

Metress, Seamus, and Molly Schiever. *The Irish in Toledo: History and Memory*. University of Toledo Urban Affairs Center, 2005.

Miller, Gregory M. *Remembering Toledo*. Nashville: Trade Paper Press, 2010.

O'Brien, John, and Jerry DeBruin, with John Husman. *Mud Hens Memories*. Toledo, OH: BWD Publishing, 2001.

Olsen, Byron, and Joseph Cabadas. *The American Auto Factory*. Minneapolis, MN: Motorbooks International, 2002.

Philiposki, Richard. *Toledo's Polonia: Images of America*. Charleston, SC: Arcadia Publishing, 2009.

Porter, Tana Mosier. *Toledo Profile: A Sesquicentennial History*. Toledo Sesquicentennial Commission, 1987.

Rockwood, John Gibbs. *Can I Get a Witness*. Toledo, OH: University of Toledo Press, 2014.

———. *Witness to the Blues*. Toledo Poets Center Radio Room Press, 1999.

Roger Bresnahan/Mud Hens Chapter of the Society for American Baseball Research. *Blue Stockings to Mud Hens: A History of Professional Baseball in Toledo, Ohio, and Guide to the Toledo Professional Baseball History Wall*. 1998. Toledo, OH: Toledo Chapter of SABR.

Scribner, Harvey. *Memoirs of Lucas County and the City of Toledo, from the Earliest Historical Times Down to the Present, Including a Genealogical and Biographical Record of Representative Families*. Vol. 1. Madison, WI: Western Historical Association, 1910.

Shaffer, Terry. *Illegal Gambling Clubs of Toledo: The Chips, the Dice, the Places and Faces*. Toledo, OH: Happy Chipper, 2013.

Speck, William D. *Toledo: A History in Architecture: 1914 to Century's End*. Charleston, SC: Arcadia Publishing, 2003.

———. *Toledo: A History in Architecture, 1890–1914*. Charleston, SC: Arcadia Publishing, 2002.

Stine, Lawrence R. *Historic Old West End Toledo, Ohio*. Ashland, OH: BookMasters, 2005.

Toledo Commerce Club. *Toledo: An American City in Portraiture*. Illustrations by John Albert Seaford. Toledo, OH: Toledo Commerce Club, 1917.

Waggoner, Clark. *History of the City of Toledo and Lucas County*. Vol. 3. Berwyn Heights, MD: Heritage Books, 1997.

"The Willys-Overland Strike, 1919." Part 3. *Northwest Ohio Quarterly* 37, no. 2 (Spring 1964).

Winter, Nevin Otto. *A History of Northwest Ohio: A Narrative Account of Its Historical Progress and Development from the First European Exploration of the Maumee and Sandusky Valleys and the Adjacent Shores of Lake Erie, down to the Present Time*. Chicago: Lewis Publishing Co., 1917.

WEBSITES

baseball-reference.com
Britannica.com
Classic-Rock-Concerts.com
coachbuilt.com
cullenpark.org
images2.toledolibrary.org (Toledo Public Library's Images in Time)
KnowledgeStream.com (WGTE-TV)
medamana.org
milb.com
milburn.us
OldWestEndToledo.com
the-american-interest.com
ToledoBlade.com
ToledoHistoryBox.com
toledohistory.org
ToledoOldWestEnd.com
uac.utoledo.edu (Urban Affairs Center, University of Toledo)
vintagetoledotv.squarespace.com

INDEX

S

T

V

W

Y

Z

ABOUT THE AUTHOR

David Yonke is a well-known writer in the Toledo area, having been a reporter and editor for the *Blade* for more than thirty years. His articles have been published in the *Toledo Free Press* as well as newspapers and magazines across the country, including the *Chicago Tribune*, *San Francisco Chronicle*, *Newsday* and the *Tampa Tribune*.

In April 2015, Yonke was named editor of the *Fremont News-Messenger* and the *Port Clinton News Herald*. He also is the founding editor of ToledoFAVS.com, a nonsectarian, nonprofit religion news site, and is the author of the nonfiction book *Sin, Shame & Secrets: The Murder of a Nun, the Conviction of a Priest, and Cover-Up in the Catholic Church*, first published in 2006 with an updated edition published in January 2015.

Yonke has appeared on virtually all the Toledo-area media channels and has been interviewed by such national media outlets as the Discovery Channel, CNN, MSNBC, TruTV (formerly Court TV), NPR radio and Discovery ID.

He and his wife, Janet, have three grown daughters, three grandsons and a fourth grandchild on the way. In his spare time, Yonke enjoys playing guitar, walking his dogs and reading.